Buoy 10

Columbia River

From Buoy 10 to Tongue Point

Larry Ellis

FAP

Frank Amato
Publications

Not for navigation / Always wear a lifevest

Boating: This book is not meant for navigational purposes. Before proceeding down any river or stretch of river, boaters should visually check the water first. Extreme caution is advised at all times, as is the use of Coast Guard-approved personal floatation devices.

Fishing Regulations: Fishing regulations often change, especially due to the complexities of managing salmon populations. Check the Washington & Oregon Sport-Fishing Regulations booklets before each season, and before fishing a new piece of water.

Book & Map Design: Esther Poleo
Cover Photo: Gary Lewis
Photographs: Larry Ellis, Gary Lewis, Cindy Thompson & Tony Amato

All inquiries should be addressed to:
PO Box 82112, Portland, Oregon 97282   (503) 653-8108

Softbound ISBN-13: 978-157188-530-2
Softbound UPC: 0-81127-00383-9
Printed in China

CONTENTS

I would like to thank the Amato family for their support and belief in me as I wrote this book, and to Buzz Ramsey who has shared numerous Buoy 10 fishing adventures with me.

Larry

To Long Beach
Seaview

Holman

101

101A

Bear River

Wallacut River

Bear Branch

Black Lake

Ilwaco

100

Port of Ilwaco

Port of Ilwaco

Stringtown

North Head Lighthouse

Cape Disappointment

Baker Bay

101

Coast Guard Station Cape Disappointment

McKenzie Head 225 ft

Disappointment Lighthouse

Sand Island

Chinook

Port of Chinook

Chinook River

Scarboro Hill 865 ft

FORT COLUMBIA STATE PARK

WASHINGTON
OREGON

Sand Island Dike

Chinook Point

Church

McGowan

Poi Ellio

LOWER DEADLINE

10

DAY MARKER

FORT STEVENS STATE PARK

Jetty Lagoon

Point Adams

Desdemona Sands

Fort Stevens

Jetty Road

Hammond

Hammond Marina Boat Launch

104

Tansy Point

Skipanon River

S P

Coffenbury Lake

Ridge Road

Clear Lake

Crabapple Lake

PACIFIC OCEAN

Warrenton Marina Boat Launch

105

101

Warrenton

104S

104

101

Smith Lake

CAMP RILEA MILITARY RES

LEWIS AND CLARK HISTORICAL PARK

Fort Clatsop Road

To Seaside

N
W   E
S

1   2   3 Mile

WASHINGTON

OREGON

Buoy 10

10

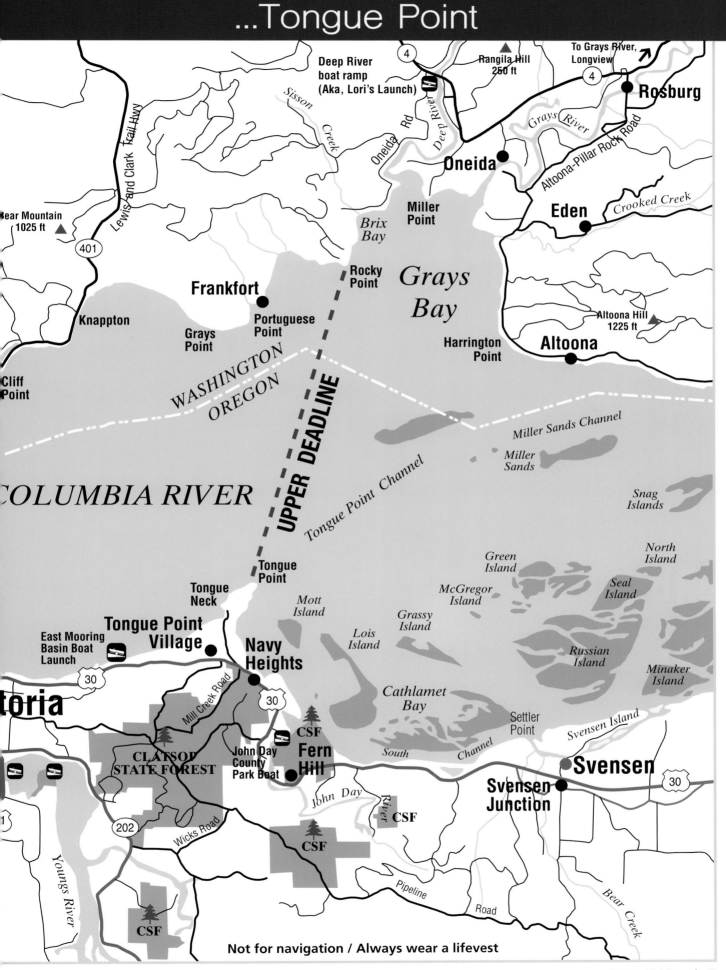

Not for navigation / Always wear a lifevest

A Brief History of Buoy 10

Frank Amato

The iconic Buoy 10 fishery has the greatest Chinook and coho salmon fishing in the world — from the mouth of the Columbia River, upstream 14 miles to Tongue Point, Oregon and Rocky Point, Washington. Historically several million wild Chinook and coho salmon passed through this area each year to their spawning grounds in Oregon, Washington, Idaho and British Columbia.

Today about one to three million Chinook and coho salmon — of both wild and hatchery origin — return to the lower and upper Columbia and its tributaries each year to provide us with some of the finest sport salmon fishing on earth.

Pre-Lewis & Clark, native peoples harvested millions of Columbia salmon each year from the mouth to far upstream tributaries. Starting about 1870, early American settlers established a huge commercial river interception fishery based in Astoria and surrounding communities to can salmon for world export. Up to several thousand small commercial river fishing boats were used, along with gill nets, set nets, and seine nets, to harvest millions of wild salmon per year.

Environmental degradation of the Columbia's watershed by scores of dams, water withdrawals, logging, mining, industrial, agricultural and municipal wastewater, etc., reduced wild salmon runs to about 10% of their original size. Through much experimentation and study, hatcheries help bring back large numbers of salmon and steelhead in the millions each year.

Intense wild-fish management reduced commercial and sport kill of these most valuable fish to a small percentage of the run, mostly by tribal fishers with treaty rights. Thankfully, intense scientific salmon management by Oregon, Washington, and the federal government has come close to maintaining the historic run size of both Chinook and coho salmon runs. The departments of Fish & Wildlife in Oregon and Washington are to be thanked, as well as the various federal fish agencies.

Today the biggest threat to salmon (and especially sturgeon) in the Columbia is not man, but under-regulated seal and sea lion populations which rip apart wild salmon and sturgeon before they can spawn.

Their populations have increased dramatically since the inception of the Marine Mammal Protection Act in the 1970s.

In addition to supporting our state and federal fish agencies we must support public-spirited fishery groups like the Association of Northwest Steelheaders and the Coastal Conservation Association whose members contribute to protecting wild salmon, hatchery population numbers and continued good fishing near home.

I hope you have many great and safe salmon fishing trips to the Buoy 10 fishery. Wear your lifejacket at all times and be extremely careful!

Buoy 10

Introduction

A large, rusty old barge on the Washington shore is one of the landmarks of the Shipwreck Troll. Exercise extreme caution here and do not get too close to the shoreline. As seen from the barge's point of view, the water is very shallow and numerous pilings abound, many of which will be underwater at high tide.

Two words — incalculable fishing adventures! Every year from August 1 through Labor Day, the words "Buoy 10" are on the tip of every fisherman's tongue. It is after all, the largest salmon run in the world!

And that makes the other 11 months out of the year pure torture for all of the dedicated Buoy 10 devotees, because it is during that time when the Buoy 10 fishery, for all intents and purposes, will be completely shut down. All fishermen can do during this closure period is dream of next year's season when they will once again be participating in this world-class blue-ribbon salmon fishery.

In the interim, you can bet that fishermen will also be struggling to get their hands on all the reading material they can find regarding the Buoy 10 fishery in order to prepare themselves for the upcoming season. This book contains everything that the consummate salmon warrior needs to guide them through all aspects of the Buoy 10 experience.

To be more precise, the Buoy 10 fishery specifically defines a particular section of the Columbia River. It refers to a 14-mile stretch of river that extends from an actual red can buoy named Buoy 10, and travels upriver eastward to either Tongue Point on the Oregon side of the river, or to

Rocky Point on the Washington side of the river. And depending on where you are located, the fishery varies between 4 and 6 miles wide.

To the neophyte Buoy 10 fisherman, this large expanse of river can be overwhelming and intimidating. Initially, it strikes as being an impossible piece of water to read. But it is not an impossible river to read to the millions of fishermen who have caught limits of fall chinook and coho within its boundaries year after year. In fact, the more anglers familiarize themselves with this fishery, the smaller it becomes.

With the tips, tricks, maps and riggings contained in this book, it won't be long before you too will be looking at Buoy 10 in the very same manner — as a well-defined piece of water that is extremely easy to read and very easy to pluck salmon from.

The numbers of salmon that are produced from natural spawning and those that are stocked into the Columbia from hatcheries staggers the imagination. The numerous hatcheries from the Washington Department of Fish and Wildlife (WDFW), Oregon Department of Fish and Wildlife (ODFW), Idaho Department of Fish and Game (IDFG) and National fish hatcheries release millions upon millions of fall chinook and coho smolts, pre-smolts and fingerlings into the Columbia River system every year.

THE WORLD'S GREATEST FUNNEL FISHERY

The great thing about the Buoy 10 fishery is that the returns of all the salmon that naturally spawn in the mainstem Columbia and all of its tributaries, as well as all of the returns that were hatchery produced, must enter the jaws of the Columbia River. It is the biggest little funnel fishery in the world! Here's how the funnel system works.

The large part of the funnel would be the Columbia

Channel marker 1 (not a buoy marker) is in the lowermost section of Sand Island Troll just off of Sand Island. Located in the deep North Channel on the Washington side of the river, the North Channel is also known as a false channel because it suddenly shallows up from very deep water into flats not too far away from this marker. Keep your eyes on your depth finder for shallow water.

River and all of its tributaries, well over a thousand miles of various river systems. The narrowest part of the funnel is represented by the short 14-mile span of the Buoy 10 fishery itself. So naturally, the largest concentrations of fall chinook and coho are always going to be in the shortest, narrowest part of the funnel, and they are going to be in their thickest concentrations in August. Looking at the Buoy 10 fishery is that easy!

It is in this 14-mile stretch of river that fall chinook and coho tend to stage, or rest up, for a spell before continuing their journey up the Columbia and to its many tributaries. So not only is the largest salmon run in the world going to be funneling through this narrow area, the salmon are also going to be stacking up in copious quantities and taking up residency for

In a good year, several million returning adult chinook and coho salmon produced from the aforementioned releases will make their debut in the Buoy 10 arena.

Hookups are quite common near channel marker 1, which is right out front of the entrance to Ilwaco Harbor. The area is quite scenic around the Cape Disappointment Lighthouse which is seen at the right-hand side of the picture. The jetty straddling the left-hand side of the picture is the popular "A" jetty, at the lowermost end of the river at Sand Island Troll. This is a great place to troll if the outgoing tide has not hit low slack at Buoy 10 itself, where you will find ample baitfish and copious quantities of coho and kings.

a few weeks — and they are all just waiting to inhale your offering. This funneling effect is what the Buoy 10 fishery is all about!

Whether you are an accomplished fisherman or new to the sport of fishing, there is no doubt that at some time during the day your line is going to make direct contact with a chinook or coho salmon. So how do you get these salmon to bite?

The Buoy 10 fishery is the most wonderful salmon fishery I have ever experienced – period, exclamation mark, end of story! Once you become cued-in to the nuances of this fishery, all of which will be explained in detail in this book, you will find that catching salmon from Buoy 10's numerous venues is an extremely easy task.

Since Buoy 10 is hands-down the most-popular salmon fishery in the world, you can also expect throngs of anglers trolling alongside you. It is without a doubt the most crowded fishery that I have ever

experienced, both on the water and on the road. So if you don't like fishing around crowds, this is not the fishery for you. On the other hand, it might just be your cup of tea, because these are the friendliest crowds I have ever encountered.

The local roads that lead to the many boat ramps are always jam-packed with cars that are often lined up several miles long. For many people it will look like rush hour traffic in Los Angeles or Portland. But don't let those long lines prevent you from experiencing this fantastic fishery.

The only difference between the Buoy 10 fishery and rush hour traffic is that one situation occurs over land while the other takes place over brackish water. In fact, this book could have been titled, "Rush Hour Over Brackish Water," because Buoy 10 contains both freshwater and saltwater that are either layered or are a combined mixture of the two—hence the brackish-

Choppy water at the mouth of the Columbia.

water connotation. These brackish conditions occur primarily between the borders of the Buoy 10 fishery, although they do occur upriver somewhat above the upper Buoy 10 border to a degree. Certainly, you will not get these high densities of saltwater concentrations near Bonneville Dam and most definitely they will not be in the Columbia River above Bonneville Dam at all. As a side note, salmon bite much more aggressively when the river contains a fair amount of saltwater influence.

You are dealing with tens of thousands of anglers who live in the nearby metropolitan cities and suburbs of Portland and Salem. That being said, I can tell you with confidence that although you will experience lines miles long at times, you will not experience the same road rage that goes along with rush-hour scenarios that occur in the asphalt jungle.

On numerous occasions, I have asked questions

or inquired about directions with many people who were either waiting in line to launch their boats or to pull them out of the water. With very few exceptions, almost everyone had smiles on their faces and folks were more than willing to answer questions or share their favorite hot spots of the day. These are by far the friendliest crowds in the fishing world that I have ever experienced.

The closest thing to road rage that you might encounter in the Buoy 10 stadium might be called 'route rage', because you will be vying to intercept salmon that are swimming in specific travel lanes en route to their native birth water — and you are going to be the person doing the catching!

And man, are these fish tasty! The vast majority of these fish are entering the estuary fresh and frisky straight from the ocean, just loaded with fat containing those omega-3 fatty acids that are so good for your heart. And that is also what makes Buoy 10 chinook and coho the best-eating salmon specimens to bake, smoke or can.

All the tools that you need to put the serious hurtin' on chinook and coho from the Buoy 10 fishery are contained within the pages of this book. It won't be long before you will be completely familiar with this fishery. In a matter of time you will be the person calling the shots, advising fellow compatriots to do things like, 'fish by the Million Dollar Outhouse' or 'start your upstream troll at the Green Line'. Whether you are an accomplished fisherman or new to the sport of fishing, there is no doubt that at some time during the day your line is going to make direct contact with a chinook or coho salmon. So how do you get these salmon to bite?

Chapter 1

Buoy 10

Millions of Hatchery-Raised Salmon Released Into the Columbia

As stated previously, a major part of what makes Buoy 10 the fabulous fishery that it is are the millions upon millions of fall chinook and coho that are stocked into the Columbia by hatcheries belonging to the Washington Department of Fish and Wildlife, Oregon Department of Fish and Wildlife and Idaho Department of Fish and Game.

Then there are the millions of chinook and coho that are released by the National fish hatcheries, such as the Eagle Creek National Fish Hatchery, Spring Creek Fish Hatchery, Little White Salmon Fish Hatchery and Willard National Fish Hatchery.

In addition to state-run and federally-run hatcheries, several tribes also contribute heavily to stocking the Columbia as well.

I could just keep things simple and say that during good years 100 million fall chinook and coho smolts, pre-smolts and fingerlings get stocked into the Columbia River every year. But why not give this fishery the respect that it deserves? 100 million salmon is the same as one-tenth of a billion salmon. Kind of gets your heart pumping, doesn't it?

I think it's safe to say that without our hatcheries, we would not have the same Buoy 10 fishery that we know and love today.

HATCHERY RELEASES BROKEN DOWN

For the most part, it is because of all of the hatcheries that there is a Buoy 10 fishery. Here is how the hatchery system is broken down. I hope you are sitting down for this.

Based on the 12-year average, WDFW contributes 28,135,377 fall chinook to the Columbia River every year, including a healthy amount of both tule and Upriver Bright (URB) fall chinook (Table 1).

TABLE 1: Fall Chinook Smolts and Yearlings Released Annually Into the Columbia River By Washington Department of Fish and Wildlife Hatcheries

Release Year	Sum of tagged-adclipped	Sum of tagged-unclipped	Sum of untagged-adclipped	Sum of untagged-unclipped	Sum of total
2004	2,556,467	14,102	62,365	29,549,737	32,182,671
2005	2,431,184	227,720	126,873	30,300,967	33,086,744
2006	1,917,050	341,797	7,100,796	15,662,035	25,021,678
2007	1,595,936	274,187	16,861,698	10,155,984	28,887,805
2008	1,767,102	263,645	19,254,411	4,586,312	25,871,470
2009	1,777,404	232,382	20,326,675	5,322,031	27,658,492
2010	2,161,719	1,304,350	21,805,165	3,579,833	28,851,067
2011	2,213,499	1,361,461	20,300,298	3,506,839	27,382,097
2012	2,120,562	850,127	21,976,532	3,231,376	28,178,597
2013	2,165,272	855,614	20,997,872	3,049,522	27,068,280
2014	2,913,644	870,417	19,700,363	3,475,025	26,959,449
2015	3,125,996	840,554	17,033,894	5,475,739	26,476,183
Grand Total	26,745,835	7,436,356	185,546,942	117,895,400	337,624,533

2-Year Average: 28,135,377

In addition, based on the same 12-year average, ODFW also contributes an additional 13,152,007 fall chinook to the same system (Table 2).

So far, the number of fall chinook smolts, pre-smolts, yearlings and fingerlings that are stocked in the Columbia River by Washington and Oregon is now up to 42 million fish.

But the count is not over yet, by any stretch of the imagination.

The National fish hatcheries contribute an additional 21,226,569 fall chinook to the Columbia River system, including a whopping 10 1/2 million fish that are raised at the Spring Creek facility alone (Table 3).

Adding up all the aforementioned figures, we come to over 62 million fall chinook stocked into the Columbia every single year — 62,513,953 fall 'nooks to be exact. And that's not even counting the millions of salmon contributed by various tribes such as the Nez Perce Tribe and Yakima Nation!

Are you starting to get just a little bit excited now? Well, there's more yet!

Now we factor in the millions of coho that are stocked into the Columbia each year in addition to the fall chinook. WDFW alone contributes most of the coho smolts, pre-smolts, yearlings and fingerlings that

are put into the Columbia every year. Based on the 12-year average, WDFW contributes almost 10 million coho to the system annually — 9,805,132 fish to be exact (Table 4).

Furthermore, ODFW is no slouch either when it comes to silvers, contributing approximately 5,739,846 coho smolts, pre-smolts, yearlings and fingerlings to the Columbia every single year — almost 6 million coho annually! (Table 5).

When we add up all the Columbia River chinook and coho stockings, we're looking at over 78 million salmon being stocked into its bountiful supply of nutrient-rich water every year.

But the count of hatchery fish has still not been fully tallied.

In years past, a goal of 2,450,000 coho were once released on site at National Fish Hatcheries. But that annual figure has been drastically reduced in recent years to only 750,000 coho. That 750,000 figure could vary more or less by several thousand coho every year. For instance, in 2015 only 715,786 coho were released on site. Next year, the on-site coho releases might be 760,000 fish. To make up for the loss of previous on-site coho releases, the National Fish Hatcheries now transfers several million juvenile coho and fertilized coho eggs to be raised by other entities. In 2015, for

TABLE 2: Fall Chinook Smolts and Yearlings Released Annually Into the Columbia River By Oregon Department of Fish and Wildlife Hatcheries

Release Year	Sum of tagged-adclipped	Sum of tagged-unclipped	Sum of untagged-adclipped	Sum of untagged-unclipped	Sum of tota
2004	1,113,092	3,946	13,887	11,688,126	12,819,051
2005	1,360,673	4,965	361,620	10,969,819	12,697,077
2006	967,717	1,288	1,267	11,799,842	12,770,114
2007	1,181,327	227,120	4,163,414	10,617,830	16,189,691
2008	1,002,240	479,982	19,254,411	4,586,312	25,871,470
2009	1,777,404	6,791	10,160,298	2,416,515	14,170,355
2010	1,780,063	528,524	10,544,519	1,367,638	14,220,744
2011	1,706,060	494,540	10,348,534	1,113,483	13,662,617
2012	1,959,067	480,783	9,813,992	1,729,950	13,983,792
2013	1,542,849	458,970	10,638,226	1,479,529	14,119,574
2014	1,678,977	447,849	9,702,403	1,795,684	13,624,913
2015	1,372,429	4,186	7,518,345	13,286	8,908,246
Grand Total	26,745,835	7,436,356	185,546,942	117,895,400	337,624,533

12-Year Average: 13,152,007

TABLE 3: National Fish Hatchery Fall Chinook Releases Into the Columbia River for 2015

Life Stage	Owning Office	Species	ESU/DPS	Distribution Date	Quantity
Juvenile	Entiat National Fish Hatchery	summer Chinook	Upper Columbia Summer/Fall Run	4/13/2015	417,995
Juvenile	Little White Salmon National Fish Hatchery	fall Chinook - Upriver Bright	N/A	4/16/2015	999,205
Juvenile	Little White Salmon National Fish Hatchery	fall Chinook - Upriver Bright	N/A	7/2/2015	3,772,533
Juvenile	Little White Salmon National Fish Hatchery	fall Chinook - Upriver Bright	N/A	7/2/2015	199,993
Juvenile	Spring Creek National Fish Hatchery	fall Chinook - tule	Lower Columbia River	4/13/2015	6,690,340
Juvenile	Spring Creek National Fish Hatchery	fall Chinook - tule	Lower Columbia River	4/27/2015	4,036,472
Juvenile	Spring Creek National Fish Hatchery	fall Chinook - tule Lower	Columbia River	4/30/2015	6,265
Juvenile	Spring Creek National Fish Hatchery	fall Chinook - tule	Lower Columbia River	4/20/2015	502
Juvenile	Willard National Fish Hatchery	fall Chinook - Upriver Bright	N/A	7/2/2015	1,803,264
Juvenile	LSRCP - Lyons Ferry, Irrigon SFHs	fall Chinook	Snake River Fall-Run	N/A	3,300,000

Total: 26,745,835

TABLE 4: Total Amount of Coho Released Annually By the Washington Department of Fish and Wildlife

Release Year	Sum of tagged-adclipped	Sum of tagged-unclipped	Sum of untagged-adclipped	Sum of untagged-unclipped	Sum of total
2004	586,161	174,645	8,378,223	2,571,509	11,710,538
2005	540,957	163,759	8,383,295	2,548,074	11,636,085
2006	655,308	170,228	7,386,320	2,431,801	10,643,657
2007	678,060	210,498	7,581,004	2,471,110	10,940,672
2008	523,571	397,179	7,324,616	2,622,519	10,867,885
2009	889,966	197,225	5,972,107	2,475,239	9,534,537
2010	1,321,639	216,633	6,909,030	29,366	8,476,668
2011	1,226,816	489,785	7,458,429	32,165	9,207,195
2012	1,417,957	142,165	6,788,072	58,228	8,406,422
2013	1,356,398	143,805	7,095,138	46,393	8,641,734
2014	1,132,835	158,581	7,392,348	507,431	9,191,195
2015	1,460,966	160,379	6,760,476	23,421	8,405,242
Grand Total	11,790,634	2,624,882	87,429,058	87,429,058	117,661,830

example, 3,213,808 million juvenile coho and fertilized coho eggs were transferred to various hatcheries and tribal fisheries in the Columbia River Basin.

That now brings the total amount of combined Chinook and coho that are being stocked into the Columbia by various agencies to exactly 81,988,525 fish, just a few thousand fish shy of 82 million salmon. And on a really good year, all of the before-mentioned departments have no problem stocking over 100 million salmon into the Columbia — over one-tenth of a billion Chinook and coho!

Remember, the returns of all of these hatchery

TABLE 5: Total Amount of Hatchery Coho Released Into the Columbia River
By the Oregon Department of Fish and Wildlife

Release Year	Sum of tagged-adclipped	Sum of tagged-unclipped	Sum of untagged-adclipped	Sum of untagged-unclipped	Total Coho Release
2004	412,182	28,406	4,606,275	1,480,771	6,529,638
2005	346,385	29,580	3,782,412	1,519,005	5,679,387
2006	335,727	26,129	3,503,776	1,725,018	5,592,656
2007	379,567	27,420	3,817,040	1,435,955	5,661,989
2008	428,545	27,775	4,319,027	1,449,733	6,227,088
2009	401,660	29,067	5,619,843	878,869	6,931,448
2010	294,052	130,948	4,958,841	22,680	5,408,531
2011	283,963	162,868	4,738,410	8,239	5,195,491
2012	332,554	112,666	4,719,459	28,142	5,194,833
2013	386,226	164,675	4,737,051	33,248	5,323,213
2014	467,151	108,704	5,324,627	31,656	5,934,152
2015	310,436	110,524	4,756,919	19,843	5,199,737
Grand Total	4,378,448	958,762	54,883,680	8,633,159	68,878,163

12-Year Average: 5,739,846

fish MUST pass through the doorway of the Buoy 10 fishery. They do not pass go and they do not collect $200, they just head through the jaws of the north and south jetties to get to the Buoy 10 fishery.

Now are you starting to get an idea of why this fishery is so popular and powerful, let alone crowded? With a fishery this productive and prolific there is plenty of room for everybody in the Buoy 10 fishery!

The numbers in Tables 1, 2, 4 and 5 were the 12-year average from 2004 through 2015 and were queried by the author to the Regional Mark Processing Center (www.rmpc.org), an organization where all of the states, federal agencies and tribes report important data involving all salmonids, including chinook and coho salmon.

The numbers in Table 3 were given for the year 2015 and were a result of direct correspondence with managers of various National Fish Hatcheries throughout Oregon and Washington.

The numerous pilings on the border of Baker Bay and the Columbia River act as cover for holding baitfish, so you can count on salmon being there as well. Anglers are often seen fighting fish in these areas, but be careful not to get too close to the pilings or you risk losing your tackle to these wooden gear-grabbers.

On a good day at Buoy 10 you can expect to catch limits of coho and chunky chinook, like angling icon Buzz Ramsey and the author did on this day at the famed fishery.

Chapter 2

Buoy 10

The Wild Fish of Buoy 10

Cindy Thompson of Salmon Trout Steelheader Magazine supplied all the angling skills she has learned from years of reading Buoy 10 articles to catch this large Upriver Bright chinook that pushed almost 30 pounds.

While it is extremely impressive that hatchery chinook and coho make up as much as 100 million salmon liberations into the Columbia every year, let us not forget that there is still a significant number of naturally-spawning (wild) chinook in the Columbia River system that contribute heavily to the Buoy 10 fishery as well.

One treatise I always get a kick out of reading is a Columbia River Compact document written by WDFW and ODFW entitled, "STATUS REPORT – Columbia River Fish Runs and Fisheries 1938-2000". When I want facts and figures regarding old salmon runs on the Columbia, this is my go-to document. Page 30 of this marvelous review states that while many of the fish in the Columbia River originate from hatcheries, "others are spawned naturally throughout the Columbia River Basin and in the mainstem of the Columbia River between McNary and Priest Rapids Dam, and below Bonneville Dam."

Having fished the Buoy 10 fishery on countless occasions, I definitely concur with the above statement. Through anecdotal evidence, I have found that anglers will often catch at least 3 or 4 wild chinook before they

A good net with a deep pocket is a necessity when it comes to the large salmon at Buoy 10, which have been known to approach 60 pounds.

catch a hatchery-raised chinook.

To me, that means that there are a lot of naturally-spawning chinook in this fishery that are not of hatchery origin, and that also tells me that the health of the wild segment of the run is fairly robust. Combine a strong run of wild salmon with an impressive hatchery program and you've got the ingredients for a spectacular fishery.

So where are most of these salmon spawning? A mixed bag of tributaries, as well as the mainstem Columbia River, are all producing naturally-spawning chinook.

In the same document, it states that "The North Fork Lewis and Sandy rivers have large enough wild fall chinook escapements to sustain unique, naturally-produced populations."

It also says that the upriver bright fall chinook (URB) s what is left of the original upriver run.

Then it clarifies where most of these fish are spawning.

"Currently, the URB (upriver bright) stock production includes natural production in the Columbia, Snake, Deschutes and Yakima rivers," is clearly stated on page 58.

However the vast majority of naturally-produced chinook originate from another area. The same document goes on to say that the primary natural-production area for upriver bright chinook is in an area called "The Hanford Reach".

The Hanford Reach is a 50-mile stretch of the mainstem Columbia River above McNary Dam, between Richland, Washington and Priest Rapids Dam. The Hanford Reach, in fact, is the last free-flowing stretch of the Columbia River that has a freestone, cobblestone environment combined with a steep gradient.

For most upriver bright chinook, The Reach is their final resting spot, which explains why these fish are so darned bright on the outside and scarlet red on the inside when they are first caught in the Buoy 10 arena. They have over 500 miles to travel to get to the Hanford Reach before their skins starts to darken and their flesh starts to fade. An upriver bright caught at the Buoy 10 fishery is the finest specimen of chinook you will ever eat!

Before getting into why the Hanford Reach is such a prolific area for them to spawn in, we need to address the first step in a chinook's spawning process — digging a redd, an area in the riverbed excavated by a female salmon's tail. In this redd, the female deposits her eggs (or roe). After her eggs have been dispersed throughout the redd, the male scatters his milt on the eggs. Fertilization occurs immediately and the egg is now called a gamete.

One redd contains the eggs from one female, with the average female salmon containing approximately 5,000 eggs. And remember that each of these eggs, when fertilized by the milt of a male, has the capacity of returning to the Columbia as a 2-, 3-, 4-, 5-, 6- or even on occasion, a 7-year-old adult.

There is a particular kind of spawning habitat that is most conducive for digging redds and McNary Dam, which was built in 1954 after World War II, opened up an entirely new area of spawning habitat in the Columbia River mainstem above McNary Dam.

McNary is located just below the Hanford Reach. Proof that the creation of McNary contributed to the increase of chinook salmon redds in the Hanford Reach is seen in the vast amount of redds that are now in the Hanford Reach that were not there during World War II. In the early 1950's, the redd counts at the Hanford Reach totaled as little as 20 redds for the entire 50-mile stretch of the Reach. After McNary was completed, the redd counts in the Hanford Reach increased dramatically and today they now number in the 8,000 to 10,000 range. Ten thousand redds in one 50-mile stretch of the Columbia is almost unfathomable!

So just for fun, what do you say that we sit down together and figure out exactly how many baby salmon are now being created in the Hanford Reach by Mother Nature's natural spawning process?

One redd contains the eggs from one female, and one female salmon can produce approximately 5,000 eggs. Ten thousand redds multiplied by 5,000 eggs equals 50 million potential lives that can be produced in the Hanford Reach alone. If all of those fertilized eggs hatched, it would be the same as stocking 50 million baby salmon into the Columbia, only it is being done naturally.

Now if you think that is a lot of salmon, think of this! There have been numerous banner years where hundreds of thousands of spawning salmon were located at the Hanford Reach. Back in 2015, it was estimated that at least 200,000 upriver bright spawning salmon made it over McNary Dam — an astronomical figure to say the least! That's too many salmon and not enough salmon redds to accommodate them!

Some of those fish spawned naturally in the river while others were seined or captured at fish traps at various places on the Columbia, including Priest Rapids and Ringold hatcheries, or were taken to other hatchery facilities. The upriver bright salmon is the most popularly-raised salmon in the Columbia River system. So exactly how many upriver bright salmon above McNary Dam are producing juvenile salmon in the Columbia River? That exact figure varies year to year and depends on the amounts of naturally-spawning upriver brights that are returning to the Columbia.

In 2015 the folks in charge of the ODFW side of the Columbia River were saying that the natural production of fall chinook contributed close to half of the fish that were caught. By my personal observations, I say that wild chinook are contributing at least 3/4 of angler-caught fish. My figure is not how many fish are kept, it is how many fish are hooked, whether they are kept or released.

It goes without saying that naturally-produced upriver brights are continuing to carve out the Buoy 10 fishery. Between hatchery and natural production, the Columbia River's fall chinook is in very capable hands, whether they are the hands of hatchery personnel or the hands of Mother Nature.

Chapter 3

Buoy 10

Boating Safety

The Wind

Guided trips account for many of the angler days racked up at the Buoy 10 fishery.

Photo by Gary Lewis

The most important consideration before you even put a line in the water at Buoy 10 is safety. The Columbia River is known as the wind-surfing capital of the world. When the wind kicks up at Buoy 10, no vessel is large enough to handle the rough seas that can crop up at a moment's notice.

If you are serious about fishing Buoy 10, monitoring weather websites, such as the National Weather Service and Magic Seaweed, is a must.

Knowing how to navigate through the National Weather Service's web page is critical when acquiring weather data for this fishery. It may seem intimidating at first, but once you have gone through it a few times the process gets easier.

To get to the National Weather Service forecasts for Buoy 10 cities, type www.weather.gov in the address bar of your cell phone or computer browser. A window will come up with a white rectangle where you can type in any city you wish. In this case, type in either "Astoria, Oregon, United States", "Warrenton,

Oregon, United States", "Hammond, Oregon, United States", or "Ilwaco, Washington, United States" (without the quotations marks). You will now receive general weather forecasts for any of these Buoy 10 cities.

This will provide information for rain and wind forecasts on land, but you also need to know the current weather report on the water. Here is how to acquire the on-water and storm forecasts.

On each of the aforementioned four pages you will also come to a small map located toward the bottom right of the web page. Move your curser or mouse arrow to the middle of the Astoria-Megler Bridge and left click on the river slightly downriver from the middle of the bridge. You will now get the Marine Zone Forecast for the Columbia River Bar, as well as the forecast for the main channel.

Anglers planning on fishing Buoy 10 should be actively listening to and/or watching all of the weather forecasts that they can get their hands on for several days before their trip. An individual can never be too vigilant at the Buoy 10 fishery. Being locked-in to several different weather sites at the same time is not overly cautious by any means. High-wind situations can crop up in the blink of an eye and turn what appears to be a semi-flat body of water into gnashing 4- to 6-foot wind waves. You should be prepared for all situations, because sometimes the weather just turns sour for no apparent reason.

Another danger to be aware of when fishing Buoy 10 is when winds start cropping up from the northwest (or any direction for that matter) combined with running over very shallow water, especially in outgoing mid-tide conditions. Mid-tide is when the current will be running the strongest, especially during wide tide exchanges. Waves approaching 10 feet or more can form during these conditions, and these waves will break!

Shallow water, especially in areas around flats such as the lower end of Desdemona Sands, has a tendency to produce these types of waves. But any shallow-water situation in the Buoy 10 arena should be approached with caution. Avoid going upriver on the mid-tide, especially during outgoing tide events, shallow water and during high-tide exchanges.

HERE IS WHAT ANGLERS CAN GENERALLY EXPECT ON A TYPICAL DAY AT THE BUOY 10 FISHERY

Without any prominent storms on the horizon, north winds start creeping up in late morning to early afternoon. Vessels will often time their trips to avoid these winds. Usually these winds will die down a little bit toward late afternoon, which allows anglers to

squeeze in another hour or two of trolling on the water. And sometimes the river is even calm toward dusk.

The worst winds are those that crop up from the south. These are the most treacherous winds that are often associated with weather fronts: pre-front, during the front, or post-front scenarios.

I have experienced extremely-rough river conditions that kicked up out of the blue. I remember one instance where a group of us were fishing on the Ilwaco side of the river and the wind suddenly started whaling on us. Crossing over to the Oregon side of the river would have been treacherous and foolhardy. So rather than crossing over to the Oregon side, we opted to wait out the winds inside the Port of Ilwaco.

When it became obvious that the wind was not going to die down, someone was sent over by taxi to the East Mooring Basin to pick up the boat's trailer and we ended up pulling the boat out on the Washington side of the river. It took a few extra hours out of our day, but we were all safe, sound and dry.

The best way of preventing these extreme wind situations is with a 360-degree awareness of everything that is going on around you. Be aware of all possible bad-weather scenarios and head them off at the pass, before they ever happen.

One of the best pieces of advice is to be off the water before the wind crops up in the afternoon. As soon as you see the first sign of wind chop, don't be a hero — pull your gear and head for the barn. Using common sense and sound navigational skills will prevent you from experiencing most bad-weather scenarios.

HOW LARGE SHOULD MY BOAT BE?

When launching at Buoy 10, boat size does matter but more important is the experience of the boat's skipper. When push comes to shove, there is no substitute for the experience of a seasoned Buoy 10 captain behind the wheel or the tiller. In this fishery, experience is king. If you have any doubts as to whether your boat will cut it, hire a guide who knows this fishery. Spending a little more money than you expected is often the wisest thing to do. A guide furnishes all of the rods and reels (usually the best on the market), as well as bait, tackle, spinners, flashers, sinkers and riggings.

When fishing with a guide take copious notes and ask a lot of questions about the spot you are fishing and the reasoning behind why you are fishing the way you are. When you hire a guide, pay scrupulous attention to detail. You may end up spending more money than you originally planned, but as the saying goes — it is tuition well spent!

NIX THE KAYAKS AND CAR-TOPPERS

Kayaks, car-toppers and aluminum boats in the 12- to 14-foot class have no business participating in this fishery. I have used these boats practically everywhere else in the Pacific Northwest without incident, even in the ocean when the conditions are extra calm, but I refuse to ride in any of these vessels at the Buoy 10 fishery and neither should you. If the 20mph winds suddenly kick up with 35mph gusts, those devil winds will throw these lightweight boats around like they are toothpicks.

I would also never even consider fishing Buoy 10 in any type of Jon or duck boat, even a 20-footer. These types of boats have a very-low freeboard — the height of the sides of the boat to the surface of the water — and are notorious for taking water over the sides, as well as the bow and the stern. In addition, the hull of the boat has a flat bottom as opposed to a deep V-style hull. Flat hulls have almost no control in the windy Buoy 10 fishery.

USE WHAT THE GUIDES USE AND YOU CAN'T GO WRONG

In the Buoy 10 fishery you will see a lot of fishing guides using sleds in the 22- to 25-foot range. And who would know best as to what size boats are the safest to use in this fishery than the guides who fish it day after day, and year after year?

Another boat style you will see quite often, and that handles Buoy 10 very well, is a 19-foot Arimas (or bigger) and similar types of fiberglass boats.

All of the above boats are sturdy and dependable. However, as previously mentioned, a boat is only as safe as the person who is using it. It cannot be overstated, when fishing Buoy 10 having sound navigational skills and knowledge of the area can be a matter of life and death.

TOP 10 SAFETY NECESSITIES FOR BOATS AND BOATERS FISHING BUOY 10

Although the list of needed safety items can be endless, I have compiled a list of the top 10 most-important safety items that anglers should always have on hand and/or make sure are in excellent working condition before they go out on a trip to Buoy 10.

1. LIFE JACKETS

As the name implies, life jackets — also called personal floatation devices (PFDs) — can and do save lives every year. They are as important to boaters as seat belts are to automobile drivers.

Life jackets are required equipment on all vessels and they must be U.S. Coast Guard approved. At this time they are required equipment but not everybody is required to wear them (except for the inflatable type which will be explained later). However in Oregon, all children 12 years of age and under are required to wear a properly-fitted U.S. Coast Guard-approved personal floatation device (PFD) while on a boat that is underway.

There are several types of PFDs, with a Type I life jacket being the most buoyant with at least 22 pounds of buoyancy. If it were up to me, I would carry one Type I PFD for every passenger on board.

Know in advance where the life preservers are stowed away so that they can be quickly accessed in case of an emergency.

Inflatable life jackets are growing in popularity and have actually become quite trendy to wear and show off.

Note that in order for an inflatable life vest to be considered a personal floatation device, it must be worn on the person at all times. If your only PFD on board is an inflatable and you do not have it on, the Coast Guard will ticket you for not having a PFD if there are no other types of life jackets available. Also note that inflatable life vests are not allowed for children under the age of 16.

Inflatables are not as bulky as the Type I life preserver and, for that reason, they are very comfortable to wear at all times. When inflated, they provide at least 22 pounds of buoyancy; some even inflate to 28 pounds of buoyancy. They are considered to be the equivalent of a Type III life jacket, but there are some inflatables on the market now that are very, very buoyant and tough; they are considered to be the equivalent of a Type I PFD.

Inflatable life vests come with a built-in CO_2 cartridge that inflates when a plastic pin is pulled or when a person falls in the water. I can tell you this with confidence — when the pin is pulled, they inflate instantaneously. I know this is true because during one of my Buoy 10 trips, a fellow angler accidently popped the pin on his inflatable life vest. For that reason, carry a re-arming kit that contains an extra CO_2 cartridge just in case something like this does occur. The re-arming kit costs about 1/5 the price of the vest and is meant to fit the particular brand of inflatable life vest that you are wearing.

Inflatable life vests also come in handy when fishing certain areas from shore, should a sneaker wave come up and surprise you from any direction.

So to be on the safe side, I wear an inflatable life vest while fishing, but for insurance purposes, I also have a Type I life jacket available for everyone on board. Children under 16 must wear Type I life jackets at all times.

2. RAIN GEAR

It always cracks me up that an angler won't think twice about getting a new rod that costs at least $300, then put a $200 reel on it, not to mention spending $20,000.00 for a brand-new boat, but he will skimp on the most important items — rain gear being one of them.

There might be an occasion or two when you don't get rained on during a Buoy 10 excursion, but I wouldn't bet the farm on it. I can almost guarantee that at some point during the day you are going to get pelted with rain. Sometimes it just flat-out pours all day. So I pull no punches when it comes to buying rain gear — buy the best gear and you will be one happy, not to mention warm and dry, camper.

Take the same pride in your rain gear that you do with your fishing rods. A good set of commercial rain gear, the same stuff that crabbers use in the Pacific Northwest and the Aleutian Island crabbers use on the television show "The Deadliest Catch," costs about the same as a good-quality fishing rod.

The commercial stuff is tough and it is made to last a long, long time. I've been buying Grundens for 35 years and have had my last set of bib overalls and rain jacket for 20 years. It's tattered and torn in a few places but it still keeps me warm and dry.

If you want to be comfortable fishing Buoy 10, you will need to buy a rain jacket and a pair of bib overalls. I suggest buying them at least one size larger because I recommend wearing a warm jacket underneath the rain jacket. I may look like a tick that is about ready to pop, but I am a warm and happy tick when I am fighting a Buoy 10 chinook or coho.

3. CARRY AN EXTRA DEEP-CYCLE BATTERY WITH GOOD JUMPER CABLES

You never know when your boat might have starting problems, I'm talking about the engine-not-turning-over kind of starting. The fact is, even if you keep your boat in the best possible running condition, batteries just have a way of going bad — it's Murphy's Law and everyone knows it's true. You may have kept your engine running in top condition, but a faulty off/on switch may have caused the battery to short out and go dead on you. A cell in a battery can also go bad at any time, even with a new battery. Anything can and does happen when it comes to a battery.

I've always carried an extra deep-cycle battery on-board my boat just for emergencies, and I always buy the biggest one in the store. And I don't use the battery for anything else either. I never attach peripheral items like stereo systems or cell phones (which are notorious for draining the life out of a large battery) to the battery — ever! When it comes time to use your emergency deep-cycle battery, you want all the juice that it can give you.

I keep my extra battery in a special place inside a battery box that has a thick wooden base. A battery that is kept on a thick wooden base will maintain its charge much longer than one that has been stored on metal, fiberglass or concrete. Be meticulous about the care of your extra deep-cycle battery and it will treat you right should a bad opportunity arise.

You also want to invest in the best set of jumper cables you can afford. We're talking about the thickest wire cables that are made. I have had the same jumper cables for over 35 years now — and I did pay top dollar for them when they were new — but they have literally paid for themselves over the years when I've had to jumpstart my own boats and vehicles, or other people's boats and vehicles.

I have kept an extra deep-cycle battery in my car at all times as well, for the very same reason. You would be surprised at the number of boats I have started that were completely dead from just the deep-cycle battery I carry in my car. Many a guide friend's trips have been salvaged this way.

4. CARRY TWO GPS UNITS

Global Positioning Systems (GPS) allow users to determine precisely where they are located and allows them to plot a course from one position of land to another. This comes in very handy when navigating the Buoy 10 fishery because you can use the device as a chart plotter and it will read out your boat's position. You can also see your boat's relationship to other points on land, the ocean or the river.

Modern-day units are accurate to within 3 meters and are extremely useful when wanting to give a coordinate based in latitude and longitude.

Having a good state-of-the-art Global Positioning System (GPS) unit mounted on-board your boat can save your life. And I'm also of the opinion that carrying an extra hand-held GPS is of equal importance. Should your electronics somehow fail, the handheld GPS will be a lifesaver.

So carry a GPS unit mounted on your boat and a handheld GPS for backup — and know how to use them before you leave the dock.

You will also want to carry an ample supply of new alkaline batteries fresh in the package for your handheld unit.

5. BUY THE BEST FISH FINDER/DEPTH FINDER YOU CAN AFFORD

A fish finder does more than find fish. It also shows

ou the contour of the bottom and warns you of any impending high spots that you may be in danger of running into, or sharp drop-offs such as those at Desdemona Sands or at the Blind Channel.

Today's best fish finders incorporate GPS units as well. The Lowrance HDS-9 Gen3 is a combo unit with a side-by-side chart plotter and fish finder.

A cool feature available on some fish finders is the "GoFree WIFI-1 Module" (purchased separately). This module allows tablets and/or smartphones to lock-in to the main unit's screen and see in real time exactly what is being shown on the GPS/fish finder. This can come in very handy at the Buoy 10 fishery if fishermen are working the subtle dishes on the bottom and then suddenly come to a high spot. They know immediately that it's time to reel-up a few cranks before dropping their gear back to the bottom.

Since you can also see suspended fish, it also helps you to determine how many pulls are required to get your divers or cannonball sinkers to the correct depth.

You have to install a GoFree app on your tablet or Smartphone. Look for this feature to become more commonplace over the next few years.

6. MAKE SURE YOUR BILGE PUMP IS OPERATING IN TIP-TOP CONDITION

It is critical that your bilge pump is operating properly before you launch your boat at the Buoy 10 fishery. It is a long way from the Port of Ilwaco in Washington State to the John Day boat ramp on the Oregon side of the river, so your bilge pump needs to be operating flawlessly.

Pine and fir needles are one of the leading causes of a clogged-up bilge, as are the small pieces of braid and monofilament from the tag ends we cut off and let fly. Vacuum up all fir and pine needles, do not wash them into the bilge, thinking that they will pump out of the outlet — big mistake. Also, keep a dedicated line bag on hand where you will keep all excess line, including any tiny clippings that were snipped off after a knot was tied. Make sure that none of these things ever land on the boat's floor.

Devon Pearsall nets a fresh salmon a few miles upstream of Buoy 10.

Have your mechanic service the bilge and bilge pump, and check all of the hoses leading to and from the bilge pump.

Make sure that you keep at least two small buckets on-board that can be used to bail water if necessary. If you can't find these buckets while on the water, look for any item that can be used to scoop water, such as a small portable ice chest. Bilge pumps can go out at any time and for no apparent reason, and when they do go out, especially during a rainstorm with high winds, be prepared to bail water out by the bucket as fast as you can put the bucket back in the boat. Been there, done that.

Relatively inexpensive manual pumps, as well as battery-operated bilge pumps, are available at marine supply stores.

Run your bilge pump for a few seconds before your trip to rid the bilge of any excess water that may have accumulated overnight, and to make sure that you actually hear the sound of the pump. Sometimes the sound is quite audible while other times it is quiet, but hear it you must or your trip is a bust.

7. HAVE YOUR ENGINE SERVICED AT LEAST ONE MONTH BEFORE FISHING THE BUOY 10 FISHERY

The time to first start up your engine is not on the day of your first trip. Make sure that your engine starts and runs smoothly at least one month before you put the boat in water. It also wouldn't hurt to start your engine up a few days before your trip to Buoy 10.

To make sure that your engine is running in tip-top condition, have it serviced by a dependable mechanic at least a month before your trip, but there are a few things you can do yourself first.

Check the Linkage

Open the engine compartment and make sure that the linkage is not sloppy. Also make sure that the accelerator cables and shifting cables push and pull freely with no resistance. You will be able to see this by looking at the linkage that leads to the engine or carburetor while pushing or pulling on the accelerator and shifting mechanisms.

It's a good idea to have the lower unit serviced as well, in addition to having your oil and filter changed. The mechanic will put your engine on the scope and make sure that it is firing on all cylinders. Never assume that your boat was serviced properly. Mechanics are people too, and sometimes they make mistakes. So have your boat serviced long before it even sees the Astoria-Megler Bridge. That will give you plenty of time to have it re-serviced if necessary before August 1 rolls around.

8. ALWAYS HAVE A RELIABLE KICKER MOTOR ON BOARD

Kicker motors are not an option in this fishery. They are used for trolling, however they can be used to get

Fishing boats in the harbor in Astoria.

The East Mooring Basin not only provides two public boat ramps for recreation vessels, but is also home to a large portion of Astoria's fishing fleet. Eighty-two slips provide moorages for both commercial and recreational vessels, and it is not uncommon to see freighters anchored-up in the background as well. Moorage availability for recreational vessels is offered on a first-come first-served basis.

ou back to the dock in case of an emergency. Been here, done that too!

I remember a trip when we were fishing in the Blind Channel over on the Washington side of the river and the main engine just stopped running. We made it all the way to the East Mooring Basin running on the kicker motor alone, and in 1- to 2-foot wind chop. It took us more than an hour to make it back to the dock – but we made it back safe and sound.

When we pulled the boat back onto its trailer the problem was fixed fairly quickly. Within the hour it took to fix the main engine, the wind had died down considerably and we were back on the water catching chinook like gangbusters.

Make sure that your kicker motor is running in tip-top condition, the zincs have all been replaced and the entire unit has been serviced by your mechanic. Your kicker motor can definitely save your life in this fishery.

DRAIN PLUGS AND WRENCHES

I almost feel silly mentioning this, and nobody immune from it happening, but I can almost guarantee that it will take place several times during the month of August. Sometimes people forget to put the drain plug in, sometimes they forget to bring the drain plug altogether.

For that reason, it's a good idea to have at least two extra brand-new drain plugs on the boat, and always keep them in the same place so you know where

to find them. If the drain plug requires the use of a wrench to unscrew it and screw it back in, then keep an extra wrench — dedicated just for that purpose — on the boat that fits that particular plug.

10. A COMPASS AND A CHART

GPS has taken the boating community by storm, of that there is no doubt, but folks have grown to rely on some of these new technological advances as a crutch.

Years ago I took a seminar given by Jeff Boyer of Lowrance Electronics on the use of GPS, plotting a chart and interpreting a fish finder. The very end of the seminar was almost more important than the entire course. Jeff posed a question: If your electronics failed for whatever reason, how would you get home?

The answer is as simple as the question — with a compass and a set of charts.

Nothing substitutes sound navigational knowledge combined with a good compass and a set of charts. Remember that GPS and fish finder units are wonderful "aids," but they can and do stop working at any time and for any reason. So take all of the navigation courses that you can squeeze in, and know how to chart a course manually. Also, keep some laminated charts of the Buoy 10 area on-board.

This does not complete the list of safety issues that can occur when fishing the Buoy 10 fishery, but it is my hope that it will engage your mind and trigger your own thoughts about how important it is to keep your boat as safe as can be when pursuing the Buoy 10 fishery.

Chapter 4

The Economic Impacts of the Buoy 10 Fishery

100,000 Angler Trips
Per Season — *Minimum!*

The Buoy 10 fishery has grown into an outstanding fishing extravaganza over the last couple of decades, and it has also rapidly evolved into a valuable financial asset. Buoy 10 has proven to be a prized commodity by providing extremely profitable economical benefits to local, and global, businesses.

Fishing legend Buzz Ramsey, a man who has fished Buoy 10 since he was a teenager, told me that the Buoy 10 fishery was now averaging in the neighborhood of 100,000 angler trips a year, a mind-boggling figure to say the least. And remember, the Buoy 10 fishery only lasts from August 1 through Labor Day. That's 100,000 angler trips in approximately 31 days!

It doesn't take long to figure out that the Buoy 10 enterprise is a boon to the economy.

Most people drive or fly get to and from this fishery. Folks from all over Washington, Oregon and California drive hundreds of miles or more to partake in this fishery. I drive 800 miles every year to fish the Buoy 10 fishery.

All businesses to do with automobiles benefit from this fishery. That includes gasoline and diesel fill-ups, new tires, tune-ups, oil changes and other automotive maintenance necessary to make long, dependable trips. As a result, the automotive industry profits immensely as a result of Buoy 10.

I am also constantly meeting people who have flown into the area from the Midwest or East Coast excited to partake in the Buoy 10 experience. Back in 2015, angler-television personality Mark Romanack and his son flew out from Michigan and fished with the same party I fished with. And in the previous year, I fished with anglers who flew in from California.

Once anglers arrive, they have to have a place to lay their heads. The lodging industry benefits immensely from this fishery. Local-area motels, hotels, campgrounds, house rentals and RV parks make the bulk of their money for the whole year during the month of August.

And don't forget — everybody has to eat! Restaurants make out big time in this super fishery, as do supermarkets and mini-marts.

The states of Washington and Oregon profit from the sale of resident and non-resident fishing licenses and tags, as well as the newly-required Columbia River Endorsement Stamp.

The boating industry also profits from the sale of new and used boats, not to mention all of the accessories that go inside them.

Factor in the price of a fishing guide, launching fees and parking lot fees, bait, tackle, rods, reels, line, lures like plugs and spinners, divers and flashers, hooks and sinkers, and the economic impact starts becoming very evident.

Multiply all of that by 100,000 angler trips and you can see that the economic impact of the Buoy 10 fishery totals hundreds of millions of dollars.

There have been limited studies conducted on the subject of angler trips to the Buoy 10 fishery. But after considerable digging, I did find one source that can back up, at least partially, how many angler trips are conducted each year at the fishery at Buoy 10. It is a study whose numbers are considered to be very conservative and grossly under-exaggerated by most of the more-experienced veteran Buoy 10 anglers, but at least it's a start in visualizing just how much money the Buoy 10 fishery contributes to the economy.

The study in question is a Columbia River Compact Document written by both WDFW and ODFW entitled, "2015 Joint Staff Report: Stock Status and Fisheries for Fall Chinook Salmon, Coho Salmon, Chum Salmon, Summer Steelhead and White Sturgeon". In this treatise, the subject of angler trips regarding various fisheries is addressed.

The Compact document shows how this fishery has grown through 2015. Here are a few excerpts from that document:

On page 68, Table 25, the title reads, "Angler Trips and Catch in the Buoy 10 Recreational Fishery; 1982-2014". Most years that were listed approached the 100,000 angler-trip figure, but there were some years that exceeded the 100,000 angler-trip figure by a considerable amount, and they were exceeded with vigor. For example, in 2014 over 107,522 angler trips were made to the Buoy 10 fishery. Due to the extremely long boat-launch lines during 2014, my personal observation is that the 107,522 figure is very conservative.

In 2001, 125,829 angler trips were made. In 1991, over 171,680 angler pilgrimages were made to the Buoy 10 mecca, and in 1988 a whopping 186,051 angler excursions were ventured to the famed fishery, the largest angler-trip year on record.

With the way things are looking, it won't be long before 200,000 angler crusades will be marching to Buoy 10 every August!

Then there was 2015, a mega-year for banner crops of Upriver Brights. Based on my experiences with difficulties finding lodging and the 2-mile-long lines to get in and out of the boat basin parking lots, I would say that angler trips to Buoy 10 in 2015 far exceeded those in 2014.

It is easy to deduce that angler trips are increasing anywhere from 25 to 50 percent. The previous 100,000 angler-trip figure would now be considered quite dated, but we are going to use that very conservative figure to prove a point.

THE ECONOMIC IMPACT IN DOLLARS AND CENTS
315 MILLION DOLLARS!

The money that is spent on this fishery will blow you away. It is difficult to get a quality motel room in this area for less than $240.00 a night. So averaging all forms of lodging, it costs approximately $200.00 a night per angler to stay in the Buoy 10 area. That's $20 million in accommodations alone.

For many anglers the Buoy 10 trip is their ultimate vacation of the year, and they eat like kings. Since most people are fishing during the day, dinner is the most sought after, as well as the most expensive meal. After dinner, drinks and tip, a decent restaurant averages about $35.00, and people happily pay it. You do have to pay higher than average prices for meals in this fishery because you are at the mercy of the locals.

For us breakfast and lunch items brought aboard the boat are roughly about $30.00 per day, so the average price to eat for the day at Buoy 10 is approximately $65.00 per person.

In addition, I think that it is safe to say that folks are spending at least $300.00 in fuel to get to and from the fishery, with most probably paying more.

So far that brings the price per angler at Buoy 10

to $565.00. Multiplied by 100,000 angler trips, the economic benefit to local and global businesses totals about 56.5 million dollars — so far. There's more to come!

■ **TOTAL DOLLARS TO THE ECONOMY SO FAR**
$56.5 MILLION!
Now you have to factor in the price of fishing licenses. Probably half of the people fishing Buoy 10 already have fishing licenses, tags and the Columbia River Endorsement Stamp. The other half, approximately 50,000 anglers, need to buy fishing licenses, tags and Columbia River Endorsement Stamps. About half of those people buy resident licenses, tags and stamps, while the other half purchase non-resident fishing licenses, tags and stamps. The overall price folks pay in license fees for this fishery is 5.6 million dollars, and that money benefits the states of Washington and Oregon.

■ **TOTAL DOLLARS TO THE ECONOMY SO FAR**
$62.1 MILLION!
About 15 percent of Buoy 10-ers are going to hire a fishing guide averaging around $250.00 per person per trip. Including tips, that brings a minimum of 4 million dollars to the fishing-guide industry.

■ **TOTAL DOLLARS TO THE ECONOMY SO FAR**
$66.1 MILLION!
Of the other 85,000 anglers who do not hire fishing guides, the following table lists the average cost incurred per person for the following fishing accessories, and again these figures are very conservative:

Bait (2 packages)	**$15.00**
Plugs and spinners (assorted sizes and colors)	**$65.00**
Divers (two)	**$25.00**
Flashers (three different colors)	**$45.00**
Cannonball sinkers	**$20.00**
Hooks	**$20.00**
Line for two reels	**$50.00**
Bait dye, brine and scents	**$20.00**
Hook sharpener	**$15.00**
Plug cutter	**$15.00**
Snaps, beads, and swivels	**$15.00**
Subtotal price per angler	**$305.00**

Approximately 20 percent of anglers who do not hire fishing guides (17,000 anglers) will be purchasing new rods, reels, rain gear, jackets and landing nets.

Rods (2)	$600.00
Reels (2)	$500.00
Rain gear	$300.00
Neoprene boots	$75.00
Jacket	$150.00
Landing net	$150.00
Subtotal price per angler	**$1,775.00**

When you multiply these two subtotals by their appropriate percentages of angler trips, the total price of fishing gear in the Buoy 10 fishery is 56.1 million dollars — a staggering figure to say the least! This is what the bait and tackle industry makes in the 31-day period that the Buoy 10 fishery is occurring.

Add this 56.1 million dollars to the already existing 66.1 million dollars and the economy so far has incurred an overall economic benefit of 122.2 million dollars! But the figures have not all been tabulated yet.

TOTAL DOLLARS TO THE ECONOMY SO FAR
$122.2 MILLION!

Of the 85,000 anglers who are not hiring guides for this fishery, the rest are launching their own boats. Approximately 5% of these anglers (4,250 anglers) are going to buy new sleds.

A new 20-foot sled — completely decked out with rod holders, fish finders, GPS units, radar, engine and kicker motor — is going to set you back $35,000. A 24-footer will cost approximately $55,000.

Let's split the difference between the two and say that the average price of a new aluminum sled is approximately $45,000. Multiply $45,000 times 4,250 anglers, and you now arrive at $191 million dollars contributed to the local economy.

Adding this 191 million dollars to the previous 122.2 million dollars, we see that the Buoy 10 fishery is contributing 313.2 million dollars to the local and global economy.

■ TOTAL DOLLARS TO THE ECONOMY SO FAR
$313.2 MILLION DOLLARS!

Then there are other expenses that have not yet been calculated, like parking lot and boat launching fees, new electronics that anglers will be adding to their boats and visits to pubs and other local establishments. It is not unfathomable to perceive that the Buoy 10 fishery contributes at least 315 million dollars to the local and global economy. That's almost a third of a billion dollars!

■ TOTAL DOLLARS SPENT ON THE ECONOMY FROM BUOY 10 FISHERMEN
$315 MILLION DOLLARS!

Clearly the Buoy 10 fishery is rapidly turning into a hot commodity and is one of the Pacific Northwest's most prized assets. If it were possible I would be buying stock in this extremely valuable commodity.

Sunrise on the Columbia River above the bridge in Astoria.

Chapter 5

Buoy
10

Boat Ramps of the Buoy 10 Fishery

Be Prepared for...
Long Lines

The Columbia River offers 7 improved boat ramps for Buoy 10 fishermen. Four are on the Oregon side of the river, and three are on the Washington side.

First we need to address the time that it takes to get to all of the aforementioned ramps, especially when the fishery is exploding as it is. During the entire month of August the ramps will be at their most crowded, especially when the fishing is hot. Expect big crowds during September as well.

Getting to the ramps at 5:00 a.m. is not as easy as it was in the past. A few years ago a friend told me to be at the East Mooring Basin at 5:00 a.m. At that time that meant leaving the motel room at 4:15 a.m. This allowed 15 minutes to get to the boat ramp, 15 minutes to get the gear together (including paying the appropriate parking fee), and 5 minutes to get to the dock. That left enough time to be at the boat dock 10 minutes early, because you always want to arrive early and not late when your guide or host is waiting for you.

Newsflash! With today's crowds that scenario will no longer be accurate. Now, even if your motel room is only two miles away from the East Boat Basin and you leave at 4:15 a.m., you won't get inside the parking lot until at least 6:00 a.m. The line to turn in to the parking lot will be between 1 and 2 miles long, and finding a parking place once you get there will be a challenge.

In 2015, folks who were only two miles away from the East Boat Basin had to be on the road by at least 3:00 a.m. in order to make the two-mile journey. Having seen the extremely long lines the year before, I was prepared for being on the road at the stroke of 3. Still, I felt extremely lucky to have gotten a parking place. It would have been even better if I had left the motel room at 2:00 a.m. For night owls like me, that's just about the time I am thinking about getting to bed. The motto here is get to bed early!

This same congestion was experienced at all 7 boat ramps. With the way this fishery is exploding in popularity, anglers will probably need to leave their rooms by 1:00 a.m. in the not too distant future. Things are certainly not going to get any better.

All seven of the Buoy 10 launches need marked improvements. Lori's launch and the Hammond facility need the least amount of work, but they would benefit from adding more boat ramps. It would also help to add an extra lane to the roads leading to the boat ramps in order to accommodate the new rush-hour traffic.

Of course building boat ramps and extra highway lanes is expensive, and many of the ports argue that spending money to build roads and improve boat ramps for a fishery that only occurs during the month of August is not feasible. Fortunately, though, things are changing.

With fishing traffic increasing every year, Buoy 10 will probably reach 200,000 angler trips in the future. When that increase happens, angler trips for the September coho-only fishery in the Buoy 10 area and for chinook and coho fishing upriver from the Buoy 10 deadline to Longview will probably increase to 100,000 for the rest of the season. In other words, angler trips upriver from the Buoy 10 area will be the same as they are at the Buoy 10 stadium right now.

I think that a good grant writer is needed to get these roads and ramps built.

7 BUOY 10 BOAT RAMPS

As previously stated, the Columbia River offers 7 improved boat ramps. Four of them are on the Oregon side of the river and three are located on the Washington side. Some are newer and larger than others, but I can guarantee that they will all be packed like sardines during the month of August.

The Oregon Side

We will start our boat-launch excursion on the Oregon side of the river. The boat ramp closest to the ocean is the Hammond boat ramp. Moving upriver you reach the Warrenton facility, the East Mooring Boat Basin and then the John Day Boat Ramp.

1. WARRENTON MARINA BOAT LAUNCH

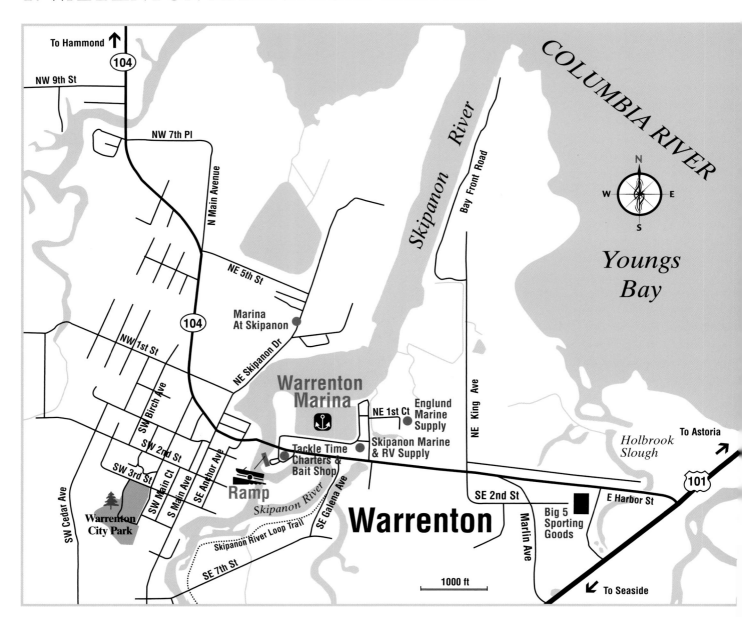

The boat ramp at Warrenton Marina is a well-constructed and beautiful facility approximately 11 miles from the John Day County Park Boat ramp, and approximately 6 miles from Astoria.

Coming from Astoria you will travel south on Highway 101 and cross the Young's Bay Bridge which will take you over Young's Bay. Not long after crossing Young's Bay you will see a cluster of signs that say Warrenton/Hammond Marina and Fort Stevens State Park with an arrow pointing to the right (west). Hang a right at the light immediately following these signs and you will be heading west on E. Harbor Street. You will see a Shiloh Inn on the right-hand side. Eventually E. Harbor Street turns into the Warrenton-Astoria Highway, also known as NW Warrenton and Highway 104.

Right before you come to a bridge which crosses the Skipanon River, you will see a sign on the left-hand side of the road that says "Warrenton Boat Launch" and there will be an arrow pointing to the left. And just so you know that you are in the correct vicinity, you will see a large sign saying "Tackle Time" on the other side of the street and to the right.

Turn left at the Warrenton Boat Launch sign and follow the road to the boat launch. If you were traveling west on E. Harbor Street and you cross the bridge, you've gone too far. Double back and turn right immediately after you cross the bridge heading the opposite direction.

The Skipanon Marina is a gorgeous facility and is very busy during the Buoy 10 fishery. You will be impressed with the amount of people walking up the boat ramps lugging chinook and coho up to the fillet tables.

A lot of guides are based out of this facility. It makes a great place to moor your boat because access to the Columbia is fast and easy. Sometimes the fishing is outstanding where the Skipanon dumps into the Columbia. After you launch your boat, you will be on the Skipanon River waterway which eventually flows into the Columbia River.

During the Buoy 10 season just follow the line of cars to the boat launch.

> **For more information on moorage call (503) 861-3822.**

2. HAMMOND MARINA BOAT LAUNCH

The Hammond Marina Boat Launch is the closest boat ramp to the Pacific Ocean on the Oregon side of the Columbia River. It is also the largest of both Washington and Oregon's launching facilities with a very impressive 4-lane arrangement located at Columbia River Mile 8.7. For all intents and purposes, you will be in the immense Fort Stevens State Park.

This place is a zoo in August, the line to launch your boat in the morning will be 1 to 2 miles long, so just follow the cars. Technically speaking the marina is on Iredale Street, but you will probably be in line in one of several other side streets, most likely Pacific Dr. or Lake Dr.

To find the Hammond Marina boat ramp look for the intersection of Pacific Dr. and Lake Dr. There will be two very large signs — one on Pacific Drive and the other on Lake Drive — right where the two streets converge, you can't miss them! Find this intersection and you won't miss the Hammond boat launch.

At this intersection you will also find bait at Wilky's Bait and Groceries (503) 861-2088. Be sure to take a right on Lake Drive.

When you get to the Hammond boat launch, the four ramps are right at the foot of Sturgeon Paul's, a Hammond institution. Sturgeon Paul's sells bait and lots of it, as well as tackle. The business also hires a large crew of expert filleters and it offers filleting and vacuum-packing services. The phone number is (503) 861-2110.

Fort Stevens State Park is an extremely-large facility. A lot of people partaking in the Buoy 10 fishery stay at Fort Stevens in their tents, campers, fifth-wheels and motor homes. But I must warn you in advance about making reservations and to adhere to the park's policy. Fort Stevens books their reservations 9 months in advance — not 8 months, not 10 months, but exactly 9 months before you are planning on staying.

Reservations for August will be made during November. If it were me, I would be the first caller in line as soon as the reservation number becomes available on November 1. If you wait until the middle of November to book your Buoy 10 reservation, the entire month of August will already be completely booked.

> **For booking park reservations, call (503) 861-1671. For more information on moorage and slip fees in the Hammond Marina contact 503-861-3197.**

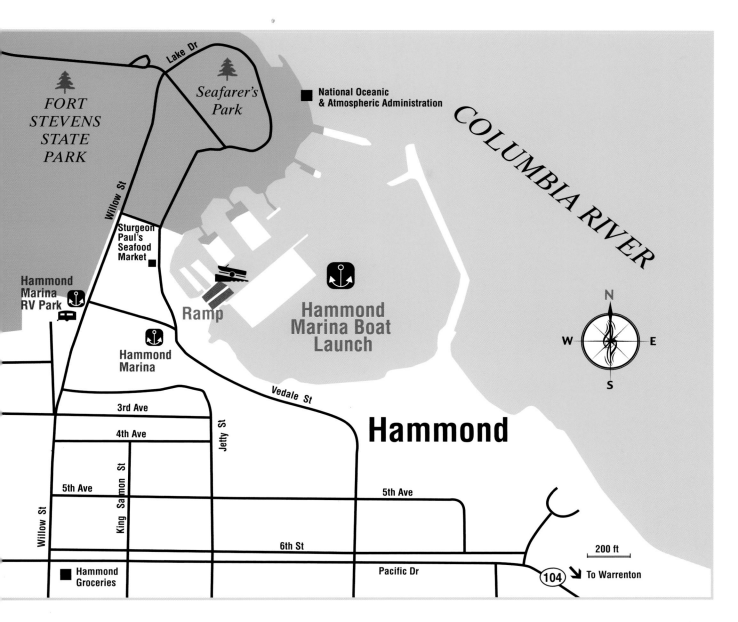

FORT
STEVENS
STATE
PARK

Lake Dr

*Seafarer's
Park*

National Oceanic
& Atmospheric Administration

COLUMBIA RIVER

Willow St

Sturgeon
Paul's
Seafood
Market

Hammond
Marina
RV Park

Ramp

Hammond
Marina Boat
Launch

N
W   E
S

Hammond
Marina

Vedale St

Hammond

3rd Ave

4th Ave

Jetty St

King Salmon St

5th Ave

5th Ave

Willow St

6th St

200 ft

Hammond
Groceries

Pacific Dr

104 To Warrenton

3. EAST MOORING BASIN PUBLIC BOAT LAUNCH

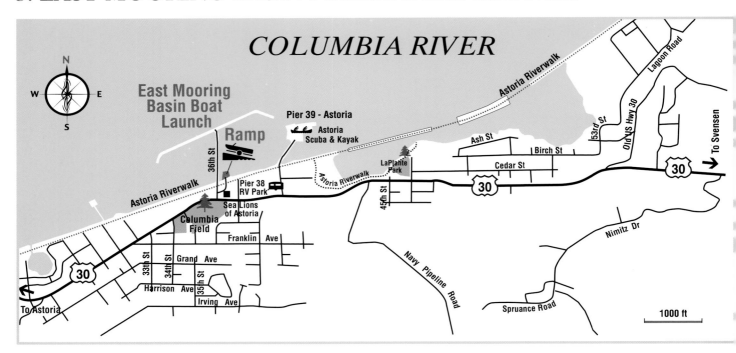

The East Boat/Mooring Basin is located at Columbia River Mile 15.6 near the east end of 36th Street, off of Leif Erikson Drive (Highway 30). The East Mooring Basin parking lot is a large asphalt lot adjacent to Comfort Suites. In fact, a lot of people staying at Comfort Suites just walk to the boat ramp from the hotel's parking lot.

You will have to cross another road that parallels the river called Astoria Riverwalk.

The boat launch is a 2-lane concrete boat ramp with fish-cleaning facility.

Use the pay box on the parking lot; put your parking fee in an envelope and slide it into a hole in the pay box. The pay box will likely be replaced by an automated credit/debit card pay station in the near future.

For more information on available moorage and services, please contact the Marina at (503) 325-8279 (office) or (503) 791-7730 (cell).

4. JOHN DAY COUNTY PARK BOAT RAMP 299

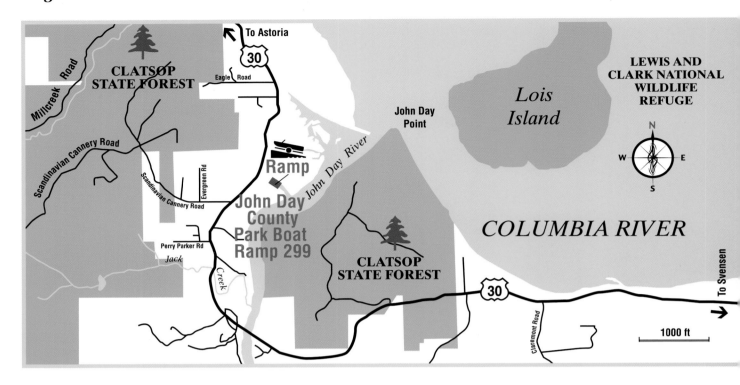

The John Day County Park Boat Ramp in Clatsop County is exactly 3.2 miles upriver from the East Boat Basin at Columbia River Mile 18 off of Highway 30. This beautifully maintained 54-acre park is surrounded by lush, green grass and also has a public restroom.

It is also located upriver from the Buoy 10 fishery deadline which makes it a great facility if the salmon are on-the-bite at Tongue Point, because the 2-lane boat ramp is approximately 1.5 miles upriver (east) of Tongue Point.

You have to be very careful about obstructions when you launch here, so if you have never launched at John Day before it is best to go with somebody who has some experience navigating through these hazards.

There is a parking fee which is paid via an automated machine that accepts debit or credit cards. For more information about the park call 503-325-9306.

The Washington Side

The State of Washington offers two awesome marinas with boat launches at the ports of Ilwaco and Chinook, and the Port of Ilwaco also offers the services of a large hoist. There is another small boat ramp in the middle of nowhere called Lori's Launch, which is the former Deep River Boat Ramp.

5. PORT OF ILWACO

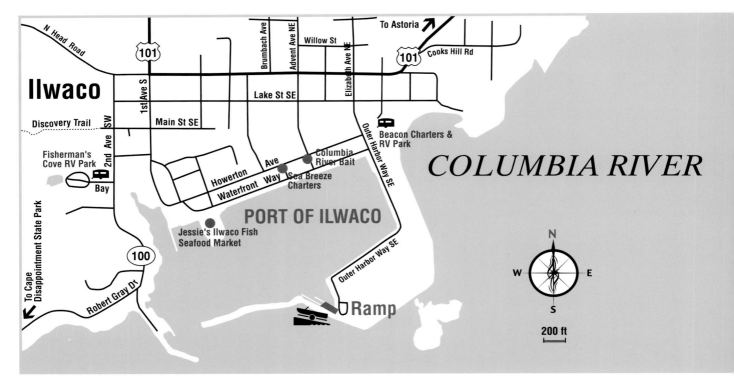

The Port of Ilwaco, which is often a choice place for anglers to launch their boats, offers a well-maintained -lane boat ramp and has ample parking places available for boaters and passengers.

Anglers should pay extra-careful attention to the all boat docks leading from the launch, which are a solid 4 feet above the ramp itself. Being inattentive for only a few seconds can lead to an angler slipping off the dock and falling onto the slick, mossy ramp which can cause serious injuries. So be very careful when launching at this facility.

That being said, this is a superb boat-launch ramp that gets a lot of attention during the Buoy 10 fishery. Mile-long lines are not uncommon here. The advantage of this boat launch is that it puts anglers within reasonable distance of the actual Buoy 10 and, then in season, it also puts you within close range of the ocean salmon fishery outside the perimeter of the Buoy 10 fishery.

At the moment, the cost to launch is $5.00 and the pay box is very small and located at a very inconvenient place near the boat launch. So be forewarned — this is not a free facility. WDFW hands out tickets with regularity at this launch, so don't be caught without paying the launch fee.

In addition, this port also offers the use of a very large hoist launch, one of the last of a dying breed.

Also impressive is the special section located at the very top of the boat launch that allows people to prep their boats before putting them in the water.

The Port of Ilwaco also offers fine dining and charter trips as well. It is definitely one of my favorite ports for launching.

Coming from Astoria, at the end of the Astoria-Megler Bridge in Washington, turn left onto Highway 101 for approximately 11 miles until you get to the Port of Ilwaco. Easy-to-follow signs point to the turnoff.

To call the port about any issue or to inquire about moorage fees, call 360-642-3143.

6. PORT OF CHINOOK

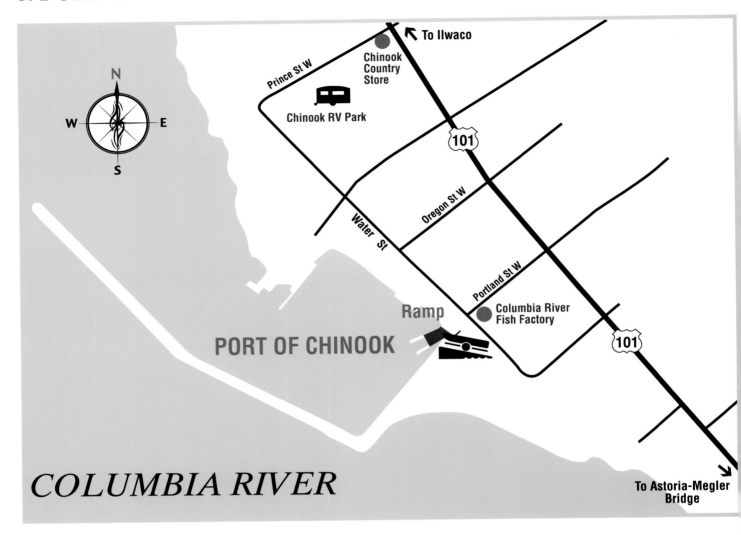

To Ilwaco

Prince St W

Chinook Country Store

Chinook RV Park

101

Oregon St W

Water St

Portland St W

Columbia River Fish Factory

Ramp

PORT OF CHINOOK

101

To Astoria-Megler Bridge

COLUMBIA RIVER

PORT OF CHINOOK BOAT LAUNCH

Round Trip : $6.00

Annual : $50.00

Your launch fees go to the continued maintenace of the Port of Chinook.

Please Pay Here

The Port of Chinook is only 4.5 miles from the end of the Astoria-Megler Bridge via Highway 101. From Astoria, traveling north on the Astoria-Megler Bridge, hang a left at the end of the bridge onto Highway 101 and then turn left onto Portland St. W. to access the boat ramp.

The port offers a 2-lane boat-launch area and it is used frequently during the Buoy 10 fishery.

The good thing about this port is that it is easily accessible to the outside of Baker Bay, a fishing hotspot bar none.

To inquire about moorage rates, call the port's office at 360-777-8797.

7. LORI'S LAUNCH (DEEP RIVER BOAT RAMP)

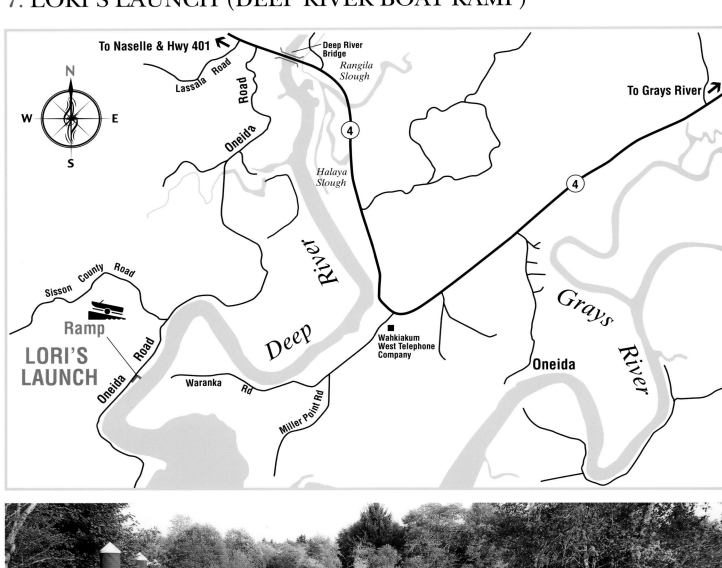

Lori's Launch, the former Deep River Launch is located off the Deep River close to where the former Deep River Boat Launch was located. The owner has cleaned the area up considerably and WDFW has added a new dock and a beautiful parking lot complete with restroom facilities.

This spot is excellent for motoring downriver to the Buoy 10 deadline near Rocky Point to intercept those Tongue Point Chinook and coho when they go on-the-bite.

Getting to Lori's Launch can be a little tricky if you don't know the area, but the dues you pay in learning how to get there pay off in big dividends. Do not worry if you feel like you are getting lost — been there, done that! It all works out in the end.

The trip is 20 miles after you hang a right at the Washington end of the Astoria-Megler Bridge until you finally get to Lori's Launch, and it will take 40 minutes out of your day. But this is a little sweet-spot of a put-in that is well worth the trouble.

Traveling north from Astoria on the Astoria-Megler Bridge, hang a right onto Highway 401. This road will take you past some great scenic spots that you do not get to see in Oregon. The Million Dollar Outhouse (sorry, rest area) has scenic vistas that will take your breath away.

After about 12 miles on Highway 401, turn right onto Highway 4. This is where you might begin thinking that you are lost because you are so far removed from the Columbia River. But don't fret. Keep traveling on Highway 4 until you get to Oneida Road, which will be the first road you get to before crossing the Deep River Bridge. Oneida Road is exactly 5.9 miles on Highway 4 from the turnoff at Highway 401. If you cross the Deep River Bridge you have gone too far, and you will know that you have done so because this is one long bridge.

After turning right on Oneida Road, Lori's Launch is exactly 2.1 miles and on the left-hand side. This is a beautiful facility, and for the moment it's free to launch here. I see that changing however in the next several years as free things never last forever.

Don't bother looking for a sign that says Lori's Launch because folks keep ripping down the signs. Just head exactly 2.1 miles down Oneida Road and you can't miss it.

For more information contact WDFW at (360) 906-6721.

Chapter 6

Buoy 10

The Importance of Fishing the Tides at Buoy 10

Reading a *Tide Book*

The Buoy 10 fishery is a 100% tidally-influenced fishery. Everywhere you fish, the time you fish a particular location and the manner in which you fish each locale is directly dependent on which part of the tide you are fishing.

With each location having specific tidal preferences, it is an absolute necessity to arm yourself with two weapons — a watch (or some device that reliably tells the time) and a tide book.

Knowing how to read a tide book is absolutely essential if you want to catch fish in this fishery. Being intimately familiar with the tides will also keep you from encountering disastrous water situations. A tide book is a type of calendar that lists all of the times that high tide and low tide occur every day of the year. High tide and low tide are also referred to as high slack and low slack. Here's the quick and the easy on how to read a tide book.

Every month has its own page, and each day of the month is also listed on this page. The tide data for each day is given.

Tide books vary in the way in which they display their data. In this illustration (above, below, page#), the month is given first, on the left-hand side of the page. Following a horizontal line to the right, the next item displayed will be the day of the month.

On the same line, there are two sections: high tide and low tide. Within each section, a precise time is given when every high-slack or low-slack period occurs. There will usually be four slack times for each day, two a.m. and two p.m. times.

Following the time of the tide is the tide height, which is expressed in feet signifying how high or how low that particular slack time period is. Sometimes during low-tide events there will be a minus (-) sign to the left of the height number, this signifies that it's a minus-tide cycle.

During slack periods of the tide, the water is going to be as high or as low as it can be. During these times, which can last several minutes to a half hour, the influence of underwater ocean currents are at a minimum. Therefore the ocean current will be as still as it can be, neither moving into the river from the ocean (also known as flooding) or moving back out to sea from the river (ebbing).

In between these slack periods, the ocean current starts moving. Minute by minute after each slack time period occurs, the strength of the tide starts steadily increasing. During the first hour after a slack occurs — whether it's a low-slack or a high-slack time period — the strength of the ocean current and its overall effect on the water's surface may be negligible. However two hours after the turn of the incoming tide or after the turn of the outgoing tide, the strength of the ocean current becomes remarkably noticeable and significantly stronger.

Approximately 3 hours after the turn of either low tide or high tide, the strength of the ocean current is usually as strong as it is going to be for that particular tide cycle.

Note that on an incoming or flooding tide, the ocean current moving into the river is very dense and remains near the bottom, moving much faster than the river current. About half way through each tide cycle — which will vary depending on whether the tide exchange is large or small — the strength of the current will peak.

After the strength of the ocean current peaks, it starts to abate slowly, ending in the same manner as it began, a steady decrease in the strength of the current over the next few hours as it approaches the next tidal slack period. As the tide advances toward the next tide cycle, the current becomes remarkably weaker until it finally becomes slack once again.

You will hear fishermen refer to "tide exchanges",

Netting a fresh silver upstream from the bridge.

as they play a significant role in fishing Buoy 10. Tide exchanges compare the differences between the heights of two consecutive tides.

To figure out the tide exchange for any two consecutive tides, when the low-tide height is a positive number, simply subtract the low-tide height from the following or previous high-tide height.

To figure out the tide exchange when the low-tide height is a negative number, simply add the low-tide height to the high-tide height.

An example of information from a tide book for a fictitious date.

AUGUST			
DATE	LOW	HIGH	HEIGHT
1	5:12	11:04	**7.1 ft**
2	5:53	11:46	**7.2 ft**
3	6:36	12:29	**7.4 ft**

The fish can be anywhere, but most will be in 25 to 50 feet of water, suspended at about 20 feet.

So on Saturday, August 29 the tide exchange between the 1:53 p.m. high tide and the following 8:04 p.m. low tide is 6.9 feet, since 7.2 minus 0.3 equals 6.9.

But the example also displays another tide exchange. The tide exchange between the 07:51 a.m. low tide and the next 1:53 p.m. high tide is 8.5 feet, since the negative number -1.3 would be added to the positive number 7.2 to come up with an 8.5-foot tide exchange.

If you're having trouble subtracting a negative number from a positive number, remember that smartphones have a calculator for a reason!

Tide exchanges come into play when fishing specific sections of the Buoy 10 fishery, and will be explained in greater detail in the next chapter.

Get several different tide books for every city and port in the 14-mile stretch of the Buoy 10 fishery that you will be fishing in Washington and Oregon.

There are several great online tide websites. One that I like a lot is called www.tides4fishing.com/us. National Oceanic and Atmospheric Administration (NOAA) also has a great website called Tides & Currents (www.tidesandcurrents.noaa.gov).

You can also download tidal apps to your iPhone or Android that are very accurate and easy to use. New apps come out regularly; some are free while others ask for a nominal fee.

Chapter 7

Buoy 10

Chinook and Coho Strains at Buoy 10

Run Timing

During August you are likely to run into different strains and various runs of chinook and coho on your Buoy 10 excursions. In the beginning of August, you can easily catch a late summer-run chinook or an early fall-run king, as well as coho. Select Area Brights bound for Young's Bay primarily make their appearance during the first week of August.

Normally summer-run chinook enter the Columbia River in June and July and are headed for the upper Columbia River bound for the Snake River and Hanford Reach areas. Therefore when you catch a late summer-run chinook, you're in for a happy meal because it is a bright, fat fish, just laden with fat containing all those beneficial omega-3 fatty acids.

Columbia River hatchery coho include both early- and late-returning stocks. Coho adults are typically age-2 fish, returning to freshwater after spending only one year in the ocean. In the Buoy 10 fishery, anglers are primarily catching the early-returning stock of coho, which enter the Columbia anywhere from mid-August to early October. But if it's a big coho year, you can catch them in the beginning of the month just fine. They just tend to be larger toward the middle to the end of the month.

Fall chinook generally enter the Columbia River from late July through October with their most abundant numbers peaking in the lower river from mid-August to mid-September.

Columbia River fall chinook can be divided into 6 major strains and 3 sub-strains. They are comprised of six major management components: Lower River Hatchery (LRH), Lower River Wild (LRW), Select Area Brights (SAB), Bonneville Pool Hatchery (BPH), Upriver Brights (URB), and Mid-Columbia Brights (MCB). The LRH and BPH stocks are considered tule stock and the LRW, URB, and MCB stocks are considered bright stocks. The MCB management component is then divided into three sub-strains: Pool Upriver Brights (PUB), Bonneville Upriver Brights (BUB) and Lower River Brights (LRB).

TULE VERSUS UPRIVER BRIGHT CHINOOK

Tule Chinook

Tule chinook make up a significant portion of Buoy 10 hookups. They are bound for hatcheries and the lower, shorter rivers in the system, therefore they are ripe and ready to spawn when they enter the Columbia. Being ready to spawn when they enter a river is very taxing on their systems and causes them to utilize all their energy resources by dipping into their fat reserves. After their fat reserves have been depleted, they start burning up nutrients in their flesh.

Astaxanthin is a highly nutritious natural antioxidant which gives salmon flesh its signature orange-to-red coloration. Astaxanthin is also found in krill, a primary prey for salmon. If salmon never ate krill, their flesh would likely never turn red. When salmon start using up their astaxanthin reserves their meat turns white, which makes their eating qualities less than desirable.

Because tule chinook are bound for shorter rivers that are closer to the Columbia River's mouth, they might work the tide cycles 12 or more times before finally committing to their upriver journeys to their final destinations. Each time they work a tide cycle, their outward appearance becomes less shiny and the red hue of their flesh progressively fades.

Working the tides multiple times like this, tule chinook make up at least half of the chinook that are caught in the Buoy 10 fishery because angler baits see the inside of these fishes' mouths more often.

Identifying them becomes easier every time you fish Buoy 10.

For the most part, Tule River chinook are larger in girth than upriver brights as their bellies are well filled out because of their fully mature and very large roe skeins and milt sacks. You also might notice their bronze tint, they appear to sport larger and gnarlier teeth than upriver brights and they have very large adipose fins. After the fish has been netted, check underneath one of its gill covers (operculum), tules usually have a patch of flesh that matches the color of the rest of the fish's flesh. After sitting in the boat tules will sometimes get darker in coloration as the hours progress. It may have been chrome bright when it was first caught, but by the end of the day it takes on a darker complexion.

By looking at the teeth, the football shape, the enlarged adipose fin and that patch of skin underneath the operculum, 90 percent of the time you can tell if you have caught a tule or an upriver bright.

Tules have gotten an undeserved bad rap over the years for their eating quality because a lot of anglers

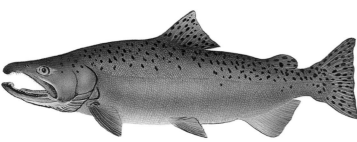

Tule Chinook

keep the ones that have worked the tides multiple times. However if you catch a tule chinook that has made only one or two tidal runs into the Columbia, it may be as bright as a freshly-minted quarter and its flesh may also be quite red. The eating quality of a chrome-bright tule can be quite good.

Most of the tule chinook are headed for the Spring Creek National Fish Hatchery, which releases at least 10.5 million tules into the Columbia every year. If you catch one of the Spring Creek Hatchery tule chinook, it is likely going to be a good-quality specimen to take home to the dinner table.

Upriver Brights

Upriver Bright chinook on the other hand are headed for the Deschutes, Yakima and Snake rivers, but are primarily making tracks for the Hanford Reach up in the Tri-Cities area, which is the last free-flowing stretch of the Columbia River. Upriver Bright chinook may only work the tide 3 times before committing themselves to the straight shot up to the Hanford Reach. When these fish are moving, they are flat-out flying.

Besides being great fighters, they are also the most esteemed food fish in the Columbia!

Upriver Brights enter the Columbia with a long journey ahead of them and they have a lot more fat reserves than tule chinook. Because of this, even though they have to travel as far as 500 or 600 miles, they do not need to resort to depleting their fat reserves or their flesh's astaxanthin for fuel. They enter the river chrome-bright and with purple backs — exactly what they looked like in the ocean.

UBs also tend to be sleeker in appearance and never lose their brilliant chrome-like quality while they sit in the boat. And because they don't need to use up the astaxanthin in their bodies as fuel, the coloration in their flesh ranges from bright orange to scarlet red.

Upriver Brights are, beyond a doubt, the best-eating salmon on the Columbia. Some people equate their eating qualities to spring chinook, especially when they are caught low in the Buoy 10 system.

When you cut open an Upriver Bright chinook, its

roe and milt sacks are very tiny, just like with springers. Having small eggs and roe is partially why they are sleeker in appearance than tule chinook.

Coho Salmon

Coho salmon will work the tides multiple times as well. In my opinion, Columbia River coho are excellent eating salmon. These fish are leaner than chinook, but they still contain a healthy supply of fat which makes them quite tasty at the dinner table.

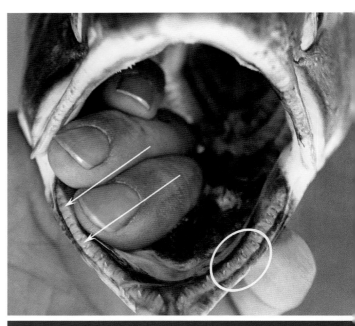

It's important to know how to identify coho at this fishery. The best way is to look at the bottom jaw, never the top jaw!

You will be looking at the teeth themselves, most noticeably at the base of the teeth as shown by the arrows and the circle in the photograph. The base of the teeth in a coho will be white, while the base of the teeth in a chinook's lower jaw will be black.

It is also important to note that some people wrongfully think that the gums on a coho should be white. More often than not, the sides of the gums on a coho will contain a considerable amount of black on them.

So do not look at the gums when attempting to identify a coho. Look at base of the teeth on the lower jaw, as you are looking downward at its mouth.

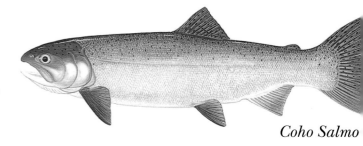

Coho Salmo

PLAY IT AGAIN, SAB!

Back in the early 1970's, Columbia River management started noticing rapid declines in coho and chinook stocks with a concern that angler harvest was declining as well. In an attempt to add more fish to the fishery, researchers began experimenting by trying out different chinook stocks from other Oregon rivers.

In 1976 and 1977, smolts from both the Trask and Chetco rivers were released into Youngs Bay in an attempt to introduce new stocks to the Columbia to help make up for the depleted salmon. Those programs were short-lived and discontinued. But as the saying goes, "The third time's a charm."

Not long afterward, Professor Emeritus Duncan Law of Oregon State University came up with the idea of using stock transfers from Rogue River fall chinook, a south-migrating stock that was about to revolutionize the Buoy 10 fishery, and set a new platinum standard of hatchery practices.

According to John North, Columbia River Fisheries Manager, green egg and milt transfers from Rogue River fall chinook (stock 052) were transported from the Rogue River to Big Creek Hatchery in 1982, 1983 and 1986. The Rogue salmon were dubbed 'SAB', which stands for Select Area Brights. Managers of the Columbia River have been running with the ball ever since and have never looked back.

"I was one of the people who brought some of those eggs back," said North. "On average, the SABS contribute between 3% and 25% of chinook to the Buoy 10 fishery."

Another Columbia River manager was keen on the introduction of the Rogue fall chinook into Young's Bay as well.

"The people who first started that fishery really knew what they were doing," said Geoffrey Whisler, ODFW Project Leader for Select Area Fisheries, "I sincerely believe that using the Rogue stock played a decisive role in helping to bring more quality-tasting salmon back to the Buoy 10 fishery."

I heartily agree. Living less than 20 miles from the Rogue River and having filled many cards with these fall fish, I have witnessed first-hand how this particular stock behaves, as well as how delicious they taste.

"We really wanted those Rogue fall chinook because they were always considered to be the better fish," recalled Law. "Now they're doing so well that we're hoping we'll be able to continue this program indefinitely."

And to this day the SAB-Youngs Bay program still thrives.

Rogue River fall chinook were the perfect match for filling a void in a fishery that needed rescuing. Their

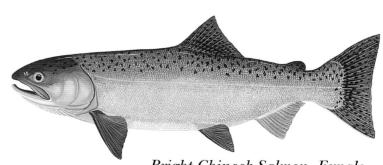

Bright Chinook Salmon, Female

outside appearance looks so much like a Columbia Upriver Bright that most people wouldn't be able to tell the difference.

When this new fishery was first introduced into Youngs Bay back in the mid-1980s, the salmon were originally meant to return to Big Creek Hatchery. The program was later moved to the North Klaskanine Hatchery and then to the South Klaskanine Hatchery, which are both tributaries to Youngs Bay. This created an economic windfall for both commercial and recreational fishermen in which nearly 100% of the fish would get caught. It is hands-down, the most efficient hatchery salmon program in the state of Oregon.

SABS provide extremely high-quality flesh because when they are intercepted so early and so low in Youngs Bay, they don't get the chance to turn dark. Select Area Bright chinook migrate south but they don't make it to Canada and Alaska to get hammered by the commercial fleets up there. They provide an economic benefit for both commercial and recreational fishermen in the Buoy 10 fishery. Their eating quality is non-distinguishable from Upriver Brights and their appearance is very similar as well, since they never turn dark. They only way you can tell whether you've caught a SAB is to look at its belly. SABS are all marked with a left ventral fin-clip.

The Columbia has never had to borrow any more Rogue River fish since 1986. ODFW has been able to perpetuate the SAB through brood collection and spawning. ODFW's goal is to collect 1.5 million eggs from SAB brood stock returning to the South Fork Klaskanine Hatchery. Half of the eggs are raised to smolts at the South Fork facility and the other half are raised to smolts in net pens in Youngs Bay managed by Clatsop County Fisheries. The fact that these fish are raised and acclimated in these areas for their entire juvenile life span gives them exceptionally strong homing instincts, making them easily caught by commercial fishermen in Youngs Bay.

I still can't help but wonder, "What would happen if a SAB was crossed with a tule?" I guess you'd end up with a TUSAB, or at the very least, an exceptionally good-tasting tule. It's food for thought.

Chapter 8

Buoy 10

When Fishing Buoy 10...

It's All About *the Tide*

Now that we have established that the Buoy 10 fishery is a tidally-influenced fishery and have set up a solid foundation for our fishing strategies based on reading tide books, we can talk about where to start our fishing journey and the best techniques for catching fish.

Remember: the water extending west from the Buoy 10 channel marker to Buoy 7, and then south to Buoy is called the Columbia River Control Zone — and that area is closed to all fishing.

The north/south line running through Buoy 10 and waters running eastward of that boundary, marks the beginning of the Buoy 10 fishery.

HOW SALMON ENTER THE RIVER

It is very important to know how salmon enter the river because it forms the foundation for being able to follow the fish. And that's exactly what you will be doing most of the time — following the fish upriver on the incoming tide, and then following the fish back downriver on the outgoing tide.

Basically, salmon come into the river on an incoming tide, and when there is a large tide exchange coinciding with that incoming tide, it pushes huge concentrations of salmon into the river.

Interestingly, when they first enter the river, they will not be pointing their noses upriver or swimming upriver as many people would think. Always looking for the most efficient route, salmon allow the tide to push them into the river tail first, while their eyes and mouths are facing toward the ocean. They will be pushed upriver by the incoming ocean tidal water, and since saltwater is denser and colder than river water, it will be flooding into the river along the river bottom. Wherever you find this flooding ocean water, you will find incoming salmon right along with it.

Salmon turn their bodies ever so slightly so that the current can push the bulk of their body upriver. You have probably encountered salmon in other rivers doing this same turning of the body to keep you from landing it. This subtle maneuver allows the ocean water to cover more area of the fish's side, which helps push the salmon upriver at a very fast pace.

The point of intercepting these salmon at the Buoy 10 deadline is so that you can follow them upriver on the way to their spawning grounds, if you are out of the bite zone you have to figure out where the fish might be. During a wide incoming tide, they will most likely have passed you at some point because that denser saltwater on the bottom is moving like a freight train, much faster than your boat is being pushed upriver. You may have to leapfrog from place to place upriver in order to be back on the fish.

Leapfrogging in this case is when an angler jets upriver to try and intercept schools of salmon that either went through his line of baits or to intercept salmon that may have gone upriver before he had a chance to put his line in the water.

Of course the main challenge is finding these places. It all depends on the speed of the incoming current, a lot of guess work and experience, plus having a few friends with good cell phones!

The key to catching salmon is first being there when they are biting, and then following them upriver on the incoming tide to stay in the bite zone.

The temperature of the inflowing saltwater will most likely still be in the salmon's comfort zone, between 50 and 54 degrees. This temperature comfort zone is another reason why salmon will be flooding in with the saltwater. This incoming saltwater also benefits the salmon by flushing through their mouths and gills, supplying them with plenty of oxygen.

The stronger the tide is — during the second and third hours of the flood, and especially during large tide exchanges — the faster the fish will be pushed through the system. They can be at the famed float (Buoy 10) in the morning and all the way up to or past the Astoria-Megler Bridge by noon.

The beginning and end of the incoming tide cycle is when the salmon will be pushed through the system most slowly, so we have to adjust our trolling tactics according to the strength of the tide.

FISHING THE BUOY 10 CHANNEL MARKER: "THE FIRING LINE"

What better place to start fishing than the red channel marker with a number 10 stenciled on it — the buoy that the fishery was named after. It is the first place where you can begin ambushing salmon entering the Buoy 10 arena from the ocean. This area is also known as "The Firing Line" or simply "The Line".

Historically The Line has always been known as a coho fishery, and it is still a coho hotspot bar none. But over the years, anglers have altered their techniques slightly so that they can target chinook here as well. For instance, coho tend to swim within 20 feet from the surface, so you may only need to set your divers-and-bait rigs at approximately 8 to 12 pulls off your reel. Chinook can often be intercepted slightly deeper than coho, between 12 and 18 pulls or greater.

USE THE PULL METHOD AT BUOY 10

Being an old-school salmon fisherman, I really prefer using the pull method for determining how much line I have let out. If performed correctly, this system is accurate to within one inch!

Generally speaking, while your reel is in free spool, or with a light drag, one pull of the line from the end of the reel to the first guide on most rods is approximately 2 feet, or 24 inches. And I'm talking about one complete pull, which means that your fingers are touching the end of the reel and the hole of the rod guide with each pull. If you want the most accurate measurement of the length of line you are letting out, then get out your yardstick and measure the distance from the end of your reel to the first guide of your rod, and do this with all of your rods.

You might be surprised at the results. Sometimes the distance from the reel to the first guide of your rod might be 25 inches or more. For the sake of this discussion, let's assume that the aforementioned distance is 25 inches — 2 feet, 1 inch. If you make 12 accurate pulls, you have just let out 25 feet of line, not 24 feet, because that extra inch multiplied 12 times adds an extra foot to the amount of line you have let out. So for this chapter, one pull from your rod is 25 inches.

This really matters when you need to know exactly how much line you have let out. Here's a perfect example: Let's say that the fish are biting at exactly 12 pulls on other anglers' rods, and the distance between the end of their reels and the first guide on their rods is 24 inches. At 12 pulls, that might not make a difference in the way your rod will get bit. But let's say that the fish are biting at exactly 24 pulls on other anglers' rods. All things being equal — such as line diameter, the type of line used and the riggings you are all using — if you let out 24 pulls of line on your rod, you might be 1 to 2 feet underneath the fish. A salmon's eyes are situated such that they are looking up, so the chinook or coho may never get a chance to see your bait.

Using a line-counter reel will not solve everybody's line-length problems either. First of all, no two line-counter reels are made exactly the same, and having different brands on board only compounds this problem.

Also, the line-counter reel may read that you have 50 feet of line out, but if your reel is only half filled with line you have actually let out only half the amount of line in feet that is reading on your line counter. This is because the numbers that are shown in feet on a line-counter reel are based on the revolutions of your reel's spool. If your reel is overfilled, or grossly under-filled, you are not going to get an accurate reading at all.

Yes sir, I will take the pull method any day of the week. If your aim is to be as accurate as you can be, use the pull method, no matter what kind of fancy reel you put on your rod.

TOP 3 CONDITIONS FOR FISHING THE LINE

As far as I am concerned, there is only one tidal time to get to this fishery and that is precisely at low slack, and it is always fished best when low slack coincides within one hour of sunrise. It is also fished best during wide tide exchanges, when the tide exchange is 8 feet or more.

There is good reason salmon prefer crossing the Buoy 10 Firing Line during large tidal swings, and you can look back on archived tide books to prove this. Big tidal swings pushed a lot of coho into the Columbia on the opener in August 2015 which fell on Saturday, August 1. Normally you don't get a lot of coho flooding into the Columbia during the first week of August, but when you have a super-wide tide exchange early in the morning coinciding with low slack, coho hitch a ride on the incoming tide, flooding into the Columbia with the tide – chinook too!

These 3 top conditions for fishing The Firing Line are not a secret, they are axioms for fishing Buoy 10 and they always will be. Everybody else who fishes The Line with regularity also knows these things, and there are only a few days during August when this particular

Outdoor writer Terry Otto finessed this Upriver Bright into inhaling his spinner by tipping it with a piece of herring while trolling 50 feet deep in the Blind Channel near the turn of low slack.

Brian Griffiths with a beautiful hatchery coho salmon caught above the Astoria Bridge during high-slack. Using a plug-cut herring flasher and a lead ball.

scenario sets itself up. As a result, you can expect lots of company at The Firing Line.

Remember: The Best Fishing at the Buoy 10 Firing Line Occurs:
1. From Low Slack to 2 Hours After Low Slack
2. When Low Slack Coincides Within One Hour of Sunrise
3. When Low Slack Coincides with a Wide Tide Exchange of 8 Feet or Greater

You also have to consider the tidal rips, which are narrow stretches of turbulent water flowing across another current. Tidal rips are often evidenced by a current seam, which can be an area of turbulence, adjacent to calmer, less-turbulent water.

Tidal rips are an important factor in determining whether coho from the ocean are going to enter the Buoy 10 arena. If you see a tidal rip during any of the ideal top 3 conditions, expect to see a lot of baitfish along those rips. In fact, when you're fishing The Line it's a good idea to look for balls of baitfish on the screen — if you find them, follow them. The salmon

Here at the mouth of the Columbia the river is wide and powerful and even on a clear day the weather can change quickly.

will not be far behind. Remember that these salmon come into the river fresh from the ocean and their ocean instincts still remain intact — which means they are going to be scarfing down as many baitfish as they can to fatten themselves up for their long journey. Because they are in the beginning stages of acclimating to fresh water, their digestive systems have not shut down yet. For all intents and purposes, they are ocean salmon that just happen to be in the Columbia River.

Follow the tide rips that have diving birds, especially during the first push of the incoming tide. Even if you don't find baitfish on your fish finder, diving birds straddling the rips means there is bait down there.

Fish-Flash and herring caught this URB for Dave Eng.

Tide rips often occur as the incoming tide floods in stronger, often between 1 to 2 hours after low slack. If you see a big tidal rip loaded with birds, definitely fish on the rip, even if you don't see any baitfish on your fish finders. Guaranteed, the salmon will be there.

Be aware that the tides do not behave the same every year; one year you may only encounter the top-three conditions at the beginning of the month, while other years they might occur toward the middle or near the end of the month. Yet another reason it's well worthwhile to study your tide books and plan your Buoy 10 excursion and strategies several years in advance; many online tide charts provide several years of tidal data.

NEVER FISH THE ACTUAL BUOY 10 BEFORE LOW SLACK

If you get to this buoy at first light while the ocean current is ebbing (outgoing), you will be in for very unpleasant, very rough and very dangerous conditions. Sometimes you will even encounter breakers if you get to this buoy before the turn of low tide — many a boat has capsized here as a result of not following this basic low-slack rule of fishing Buoy 10.

The tide times listed in the tide books may not match the actual time of low slack as dictated by Mother Nature. In fact, the time might vary anywhere from 15 to 60 minutes later than what your tide book states, so approach The Line with caution and respect.

I heartily recommend finding an online tide chart or tide table booklet for the Ilwaco area, since Ilwaco is the closest location to the actual Buoy 10. Even so, the actual time of low tide could still vary anywhere between 15 to 60 minutes.

If you have your heart set on fishing the red Buoy 10 channel marker (as thousands of people do every year), and the water around you looks like you're sitting inside a kettle of boiling soup, fish another location close by. You could fish the Ilwaco area and wing dams numbers 1, 3 and 5 in front of Baker Bay, wait another half hour and then come back and try Buoy 10 again.

When the water starts to flatten out, then you know you have reached this area during low slack. Another sign that you've reached this area at the right time — about 500 boats trolling all around you. The wakes caused by this heavy boat traffic can cause this area to get mighty sloppy, so be careful.

TROLLING UPRIVER FROM THE NUMBER 10 BUOY

During the first hour or so of low slack, the current might not be pushing very hard, so you can basically troll in any direction. But sometimes you won't have any choice but to go with the flow if several hundred boats are trolling in the same direction.

This is not necessarily a bad thing. If you see boats all doing the same thing, then simply follow the leader and go with the flow — they must be doing something right! If you happen to see a few nets in the air, so much the better — the bite is on! And you will also have the confidence of knowing that fish are moving through the system.

Generally speaking, you can forward troll from channel marker number 10 for the first hour or so after low tide. And if that is what everyone else is doing, then you will know which technique to deploy. If this is your first time fishing The Line, don't get into the thickest part of the trolling fleet right away. Get in the back of the line and watch how the locals handle things such as landing fish and navigating through the area when they have a fish on. You will probably be trolling over the same fish anyway. Or in the case of an incoming tide at Buoy 10, they will be coming to you.

You might start out at low slack by forward trolling in several different directions when the current is weak, but as the current gets stronger, you will use another technique popular on The Line (and elsewhere in this fishery). As the tide starts to flood in stronger, usually one hour following low slack and during the first half of the incoming tide, the best strategy is to turn your bow to the ocean, which is west, and hold your boat in the current with your trolling motor. This is known as hover fishing and allows you to hold your position in one spot while waiting for the incoming chrome missiles to come to you.

Since the fish will be traveling rapidly through the incoming tide, with their eyes pointed toward the ocean, all these incoming fish will get a chance to see your setup.

If you see most of the boats pointing their bows toward the ocean one hour after low slack, you will know exactly what they are doing. Some boats will be holding steady in the current, while others will be slowly inching their way upriver — a very effective Buoy 10 technique called back-trolling. If you see everybody deploying this tactic, then join in on this go-to fishing method.

Generally speaking, the actual Buoy 10 area will fish well for the first 2 hours following low tide. After that, back-troll from Buoy 10 through Buoys 12, 14, 20, 22 and even on into Hammond. However, if you did not see many, or any, nets going into the water during this 2-hour troll the fish might have moved into the river at a different location, or they somehow managed to skirt around your bait.

From here you have two choices...

Now that you are well into the second half of the incoming tide with a fairly-strong current, you could continue to back-troll further upriver and then hover-fish when you get to the Hammond area. Hammond can often be on fire for hover fishing during the second half of the incoming tide.

As the tide starts to soften, you can then switch to forward trolling all the way through Warrenton and onto the Green Line, which is a bunch of green buoys straddling the south shipping channel and the Young's Bay Control Zone. You can forward troll until you get to or go beyond the Astoria-Megler Bridge, always keeping Desdemona Sands on your left, or on the north side of you.

The second choice you can make is to cut over from Buoy 16 to Chinook Point on the Washington side of the river and forward troll upstream through the Church Hole, which is just downstream from the Astoria-Megler Bridge. You can keep forward trolling underneath the bridge and then troll the last hour of the flood through the Blind Channel.

The point in cutting across to the Washington side from Buoy 16 is to avoid running across Desdemona Sands, a dangerous shallow-water hazard. By cutting across the river from Buoy 16, you should remain well downriver from the lowest boundary (the west end) of Desdemona Sands which is marked with a three-legged structure called The Checkerboard.

Whatever your fishing tactics may be, time your ride on the incoming tide so that you will be at or above the Astoria-Megler Bridge when high slack rolls around.

On large tides, the troll from the actual Buoy 10 to the Astoria-Megler Bridge might take less time than you think. On a wide tide exchange, and if all the stars are in perfect alignment, it should take about 6 hours or less to conduct this particular troll.

Remember that fishing on the incoming tide on a wide tide exchange of 8 feet or more is only a guideline. However on most days in August you will not be able to do this, so you will have to take what you can get as far as tide exchanges go. Always strive to be at The Line within one hour of sunrise and also at low slack, regardless of the tide exchanges.

LOCATE THE SALTWATER-FRESHWATER BREAK

To fish the lower Buoy 10 area effectively you will need to find the break between the denser saltwater and less-dense freshwater on your fish finder in order to know at what depth to put your bait or spinner.

To do this, turn up the gain on your fish finder until you can see the definite break where the incoming saltwater meets the river's freshwater. The break will either look like a line near the bottom of the screen, or the bottom of the screen will show many feet of static while the center to the top of the screen will not show any static at all.

Ocean water is far more dense and weighs considerably more than fresh river water, so you are going to find incoming ocean water on the bottom.

For chinook, put your bait or spinner a few feet above the saltwater break, which will likely be more than 10 feet off of the bottom. Salmon will see your bait and swim upward to the freshwater to engulf your offering.

For coho, run your baits much shallower.

If you put your bait on the bottom while fishing The Line it will be immediately torn to shreds by the strong ocean current. During the third hour of an incoming tide cycle the current is so strong it will pull drag off of your reel, even when you have your drag tightened down.

On the other hand, you can and should troll on the bottom or very close to the bottom when performing a downstream troll on an outgoing tide, when there is no incoming ocean water influence.

THE BEST DEPTH TO FISH THE LINE

Let's say that you have just arrived at The Line and low slack, sunrise and the tide exchanges are all perfectly lined up. You know that fish are flooding in following the bottom contour because you can see the large arches on your depth-finder screen. But that does not mean you should be fishing right on the bottom — not on an incoming tide at The Firing Line anyway. You might fish on the bottom during an outgoing tide (and you probably will), but you will never fish on the bottom during a strong incoming tide, especially at The Line!

If you fished on the bottom during a strong incoming tide, your bait would get ripped to shreds by the super-strong incoming ocean current, especially toward the lower end of the Buoy 10 fishery. As a matter of fact, the current is so strong during the middle of a wide incoming tide cycle that you will not be able to hold your rod without line coming off of the reel. You will think that you have hooked a whale when in fact the incoming ocean current has grabbed hold of your line. So during these circumstances you will want to be fishing a foot or two just above the incoming saltwater, which can be verified on your fish finder.

I like to run a diver-and-bait or a diver-and-spinner setup; both will be explained in Chapter 13. Run your setups between 6 and 16 pulls for coho and between 8 and 24 pulls for chinook. Add a couple of pulls when you get up to the Hammond Area.

Chapter 9

Buoy 10

The Most Popular...

Tide Cycle to Fish

Most fishing guides would agree that the best time to have your line in the water, especially in the Astoria-Megler Bridge area, is during high slack and on the first half of the outgoing tide. If high slack just happens to coincide with the crack of dawn, you've hit paydirt. To most experienced Buoy 10-ers, this is not just the best tide to fish, it is the only tide to fish!

When the tide reaches high slack the salmon have, for the most part, been pushed into the river up to or past the Astoria-Megler Bridge by a strong incoming tide. At the turn of high tide, you are going to be fishing either just above or below the Astoria-Megler Bridge, adjacent to Desdemona Sands, either in the north channel on the Washington side or the south channel on the Oregon side.

On the Washington side you might be trolling at Million Dollar Outhouse, Shipwreck, or inside the Blind Channel or Church Hole.

Ebb tide, also known as the outgoing tide, is when the tide reaches high slack and then starts to flow back to sea. During this time, salmon will turn around and face upstream, pointing their noses into the current. This is the time to perform a downstream troll.

The rule of thumb at Buoy 10 is that the best bite of the day is at the turn of high tide and through the first half of the ebb.

For the sake of discussion, let's put ourselves back at low slack at the number 10 buoy starting at sunrise. You started fishing at 5:30 a.m. at Buoy 10 right at low slack, and you have been deploying a combination of back-trolling and forward-trolling techniques during the last half of the incoming tide. You are now just upriver from the Astoria-Megler Bridge and have the rare opportunity of fishing this special turn of the tide at or around 11:30 am.

This scenario would set you up for fishing the Buoy 10 daily double — fishing both low slack and the incoming tide, and high slack and the outgoing tide in the same day.

Given the above circumstances, by 11:30 a.m. or 12:00 p.m. the wind should not be too much of a problem, so you might be able to fish the first or second hour of the outgoing tide. Of course if you see any signs of west winds with white caps, make tracks for home — and the sooner, the better.

That being said, most guides prefer fishing the first half of the outgoing high tide, especially when the aforementioned tide occurs within one hour of sunrise and when the tide exchange is less than 7 feet, with a 4- to 5-foot tide exchange being ideal.

I agree whole-heartedly with this practice. The argument here is that during these "softer" tide exchanges, fish tend to stack up and hold up in the estuary for longer periods of time. And the argument definitely holds water. It is almost a guarantee that most of the salmon that came in with the large incoming tide are going to be at or above the Astoria-Megler Bridge by the time high tide rolls around. On softer tide exchanges, the salmon will not tend to ride a soft tide back out to sea.

With a lot of soft tides in the 3.5- to 5-foot range, salmon tend to stack up in the bay above and/or below the Astoria-Megler Bridge, and they will often stick around for several days. Hands down, this is my favorite time to fish — at high slack and the first half of the ebb, and after several days of soft tides. But with salmon sticking around during soft tides, you can often bag these fish by only having to work a few spots near the bridge. I live for these types of conditions.

The old saying that you should be low in the river near Ilwaco or Buoy 10 on a low tide does not always hold water. During the before-mentioned tide conditions you can whack chinook as you approach low tide on the last half of the ebb while fishing the Blind Channel, which is especially favorable during the last hour of the ebb or even when approaching slack conditions. The turn of low to high can also be productive in these spots.

Indeed, when I look back at my logs, most of the fish that I caught at Buoy 10 were hooked during the first half of the outgoing tide on low-tide exchanges. The rest of my hookups came during the last half of the outgoing tide, at low slack, or during the first 2 hours of the incoming tide, and again on low-tide exchanges.

Generally speaking, anglers will follow the fish all the way downriver on the entire outgoing tide starting from the Blind Channel and ending up in front of Baker Bay and breakwater dolphin number 1, especially during a wide tide exchange.

Plan your Buoy 10 trip on a series of consecutive low-tide exchanges, where the fishing up at the bridge should be stellar on both tide cycles.

There are only a handful of days out of the month when high slack occurs within one hour after sunrise. But even though this only occurs a few times a month, you can plan your trip to match this particular tide cycle as well. The folks who put on the Buoy 10 Challenge do exactly that every year!

The point here is that you want your rods in the water with either bait or spinners attached during high slack and during the first half of the ebb, no matter what the time of day. You never, ever want to miss fishing the first half of the outgoing tide.

Buoy 10 guide Bill Monroe, Jr. holds a large Upriver Bright caught by outdoor writer Josiah Darr while fishing in the 2015 Buoy 10 Challenge. The Challenge, an annual tournament and fundraiser, is hosted by the National Sportfishing Industry Association, an organization that helps to promote sportfishing opportunities in Washington, Oregon and Idaho.

Gary Lewis with the best coho of the day. These fish are at the prime of their lives in top condition and they fight hard!

Chapter 10

Buoy 10

The Practical Side
of Fishing Buoy 10

The Partial *Tide Cycle*

Not everybody will be able to fish a complete tide cycle down at the number 10 buoy at low slack, on the incoming tide, during a wide tide exchange, and within one hour of sunrise. Nor is it realistic to assume that all anglers will be able to fish a complete tide cycle up at the Astoria-Megler Bridge at high slack, on an outgoing tide, during a soft tide exchange, and within one hour of daylight.

It's really nice when all of these things do happen together, but these ideal tidal conditions might only occur 7 days out of the entire month of August — tops!

Realistically though, everyone can hope to fish at least one or two partial tide cycles that contain at least some of these tidal conditions, and they can fish during these partial tide cycles for at least 3 weeks during August. These are the more common conditions that anglers can expect to find during most of the Buoy 10 fishery. They are the bread-and-butter days of the fishery.

There are two requirements however that anglers can strive for: being on the river within one hour after first legal light and fishing during the last hour of one tide cycle and the first hour of the next tide cycle. You can expect to encounter this situation at least one time during the day — don't miss it!

For some reason, the period of time from one hour before any slack tide to one hour after the turn of that particular slack tide really gets fish turned on, and they go on-the-bite like gangbusters. So if you can fish any turn of the tide, you will have a lot going your way.

It is also realistic to assume that unless a freak squall appears out of the blue, anglers can be on the water at some point during the day when at least one slack period occurs, whether it is high slack or low slack. Granted, those conditions might not occur at the crack of dawn, which would be ideal, but you always want to have your rods locked and loaded and in the water during these stellar two-hour fishing periods.

Worst-case scenario would be if high slack falls around 3:30 a.m. and 3:30 p.m. During these particular tidal periods you will usually not be able to experience the first half of the outgoing tide because 3:30 a.m. is before first legal light, and the notorious west winds or, heaven forbid, the dreaded south winds are kicking up around 3:30 p.m. There are those rare days when the Columbia might not get any wind in the afternoon, but I wouldn't bet the farm on it.

The fact of the matter is that for three weeks out of the month of August you are only going to be able to fish during a partial set of ideal tide conditions, and you are going to have to milk them for all they are worth.

Here is an example of how anglers can experience one or more partial tide cycles: if high slack falls at 3:30 a.m., you will be able to experience at least part of the first half of the ebb and the complete last half of the ebb, say from 5:30 a.m. until low slack occurs at 9:30 a.m. — which isn't a bad ebb tide to have on any day to perform your downstream troll.

When the tide changes from low slack and starts flooding up the river you still have another three hours of prime incoming tide to fish. That's seven hours to experience parts of both the outgoing tide and incoming tide during partial tide cycles.

Given that high slack occurred at 3:30 a.m., low slack will be occurring at 9:30 a.m., and high slack is slated to go down at 3:30 p.m., how would you adjust your fishing tactics for the day to suit this particular tidal situation?

First, make an educated guess as to where the bulk of the fish are going to be during any particular portion of the tide. Take the 3:30 a.m. high tide for example. You will be able to perform a downstream troll on a partial outgoing tide, say from 5:30 a.m. until low slack occurs at 9:30 a.m. You have also checked your tide book and found that there's a wide tide exchange between these two tides as well. You now have a solid foundation for performing your strategy of the day.

Since the bulk of the salmon were probably up at the Astoria-Megler Bridge on the early-morning high tide, you will now be following the fish downriver with a downstream troll. You will have to find where these fish have travelled to since 3:30 a.m., figure out where most of them would be after traveling two hours downriver after the turn of high tide, assuming that the bulk of them were up at the Astoria-Megler Bridge at high slack. Then launch your boat and head down to these places to intercept the fish.

On a wide tidal exchange, salmon at the Astoria-Megler Bridge can ride the tide back to sea on one tide cycle. Based on an average 6-hour tide cycle, and after figuring that they have traveled two hours downriver, you can now break up the fishery into sections and make a deduction that the fish are probably one-third of the way from the Astoria-Megler Bridge down to the number 10 buoy.

With help from your compass and map you have discovered two good possibilities for where the fish might be: toward the west end of the Church Hole on the Washington side, or they could be off the Sawdust Pile on the Oregon side. You fire up your engine and head downriver on the Washington side of the river, only to find that there are several hundred boats congregating on the lower one-third of the Church Hole, and several boats already have nets out.

If you had decided to head down the Oregon side of the river, you would also have found several hundred boats performing a downstream troll off the Sawdust Pile, with multiple anglers fighting fish as well.

This is why sometimes, especially if you are new to

his fishery, it is often best not to be the first boat on the water. It really pays off to wait at least 30 minutes to see where the bulk of the fleet is going to fish under these types of conditions.

More importantly, note where the fishing guides are. You will easily recognize them because their boats will be wrapped like NASCAR cars, each boat sporting their contact information and sponsors aplenty.

A second scenario you might encounter is when the tide exchange between the 3:30 a.m. high tide and the 9:30 a.m. low slack tide is under 5 feet, and the tidal exchange between the 9:30 a.m. low tide and the next 3:30 p.m. high tide is less than 5 feet as well. Under these soft tidal conditions, expect to find chinook and coho closer to the Astoria-Megler Bridge near places like Million Dollar Outhouse, Shipwreck, and the Blind Channel.

The main point here is that the Buoy 10 fishery can be successfully fished every day in August and under any set of tidal conditions. The only thing holding anyone back in this fishery is inclement weather.

There are numerous other tidal situations that occur during Buoy 10's bread-and-butter days in August, but now you can figure out for yourself where the fish will be on any given day, because everything in the Buoy 10 game depends on following the fish, and sometimes the anglers.

Fishing Buoy 10 involves making a series of educated guesses as to where you think the fish will be at any given time, based on their mode of traveling under a specific set of tidal conditions.

An angler does battle with a coho in choppy water while another fisherman checks his line to avoid hooking the line.

Photo by Gary Lewis

Chapter 11

Buoy 10

The Fishing...

Holes

As with any fishery, Buoy 10 features a plethora of well-known trolls and favored fishing spots. There are enough fishing holes to keep the fully autonomous Buoy 10 warrior well armed for many battles during the month of August.

1. THE NUMBER 10 BUOY

This is the westernmost fishing boundary of the Buoy 10 fishery. When the gun goes off, the Buoy 10 starting line will be the first place where anglers can start intercepting chinook and coho as they make their way into the Columbia River. Make sure you arrive here at low slack (never before) and troll upstream on the incoming tide. It is best fished when the tide exchange is greater than 8 feet.

During the first hour of the incoming tide, you can forward troll in any direction but as the tide starts to flood in stronger, point your bow toward the ocean and hold your boat in the current, waiting for those fresh silvers and kings to come to you. As the tide gets even stronger, allow your boat to slip upriver ever so slightly, a technique called back-trolling.

Back-troll for about 1 1/2 hours through Buoy numbers 12, and 14 and 20, then leapfrog up to Hammond and hold your boat in the current there — waiting for the mass of fish that passed you by at the number 10 channel marker to hammer your offering.

The depth at Buoy 10 will range from 30 to 50 feet. Fish will be suspended above the saltwater/freshwater break; use fish finders to determine where this break is and then put your baits or spinners at or above this break. The ideal depth to fish will vary between 8 to 12 pulls for coho, and up to 20 pulls for chinook.

Use Delta Divers or Double Deep Six Divers with a large Fish Flash flasher attached to the diver. Whole and cut-plug herring both work great, as do red-and-white Toman Thumper spinners. Look for current seams, tidal rips and diving birds, all good signs that baitfish are in the area.

Buoy 10 with a seal taking a nap on deck.

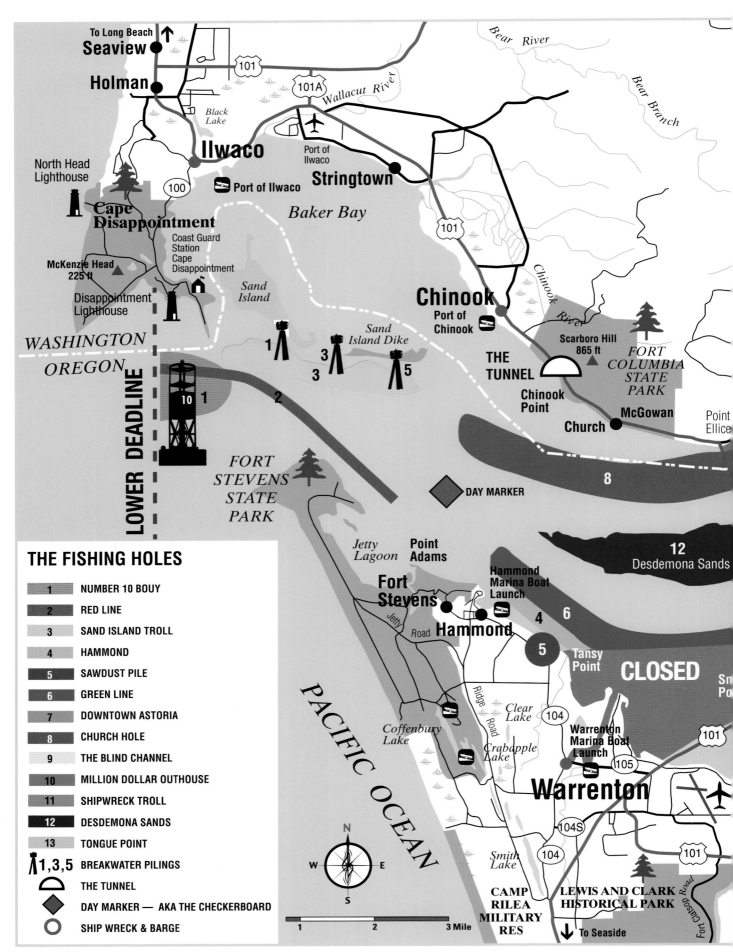

THE FISHING HOLES

1	NUMBER 10 BOUY
2	RED LINE
3	SAND ISLAND TROLL
4	HAMMOND
5	SAWDUST PILE
6	GREEN LINE
7	DOWNTOWN ASTORIA
8	CHURCH HOLE
9	THE BLIND CHANNEL
10	MILLION DOLLAR OUTHOUSE
11	SHIPWRECK TROLL
12	DESDEMONA SANDS
13	TONGUE POINT

1,3,5 BREAKWATER PILINGS

THE TUNNEL

DAY MARKER — AKA THE CHECKERBOARD

SHIP WRECK & BARGE

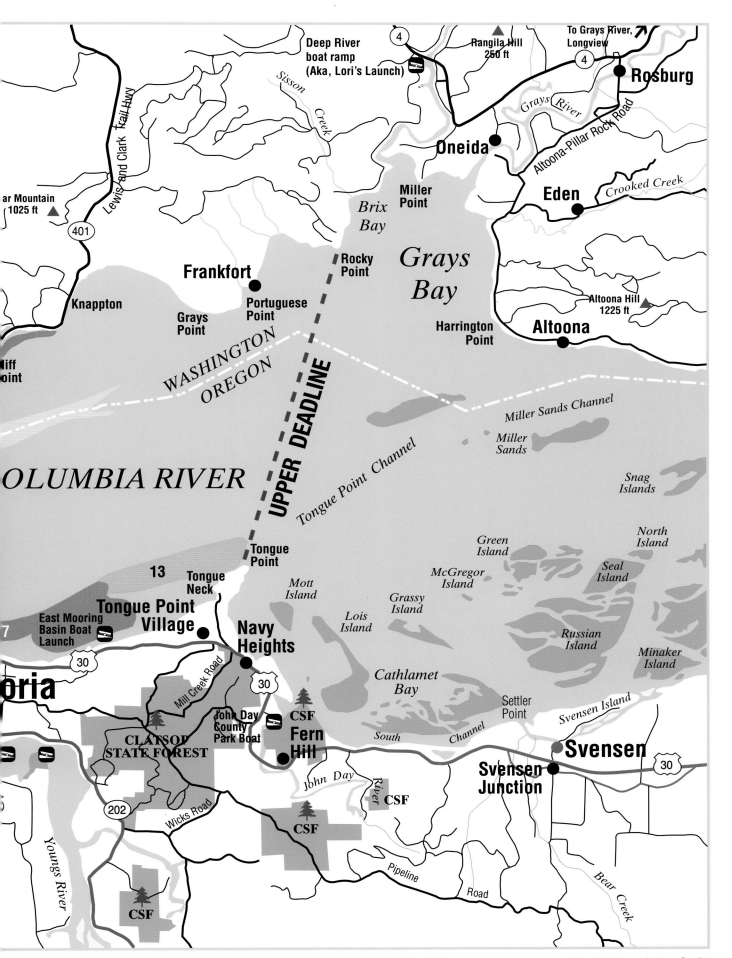

To Grays River, Longview

4

Deep River boat ramp (Aka, Lori's Launch)

Sisson Creek

Rangila Hill 250 ft

Grays River

Rosburg

Oneida

Eden

Crooked Creek

Altoona-Pillar Rock Road

Miller Point

Brix Bay

Grays Bay

Rocky Point

Frankfort

Knappton

Grays Point

Portuguese Point

Altoona Hill 1225 ft

Harrington Point

Altoona

ar Mountain 1025 ft

401

liff oint

WASHINGTON

OREGON

UPPER DEADLINE

Miller Sands Channel

Miller Sands

Tongue Point Channel

Snag Islands

OLUMBIA RIVER

North Island

Green Island

McGregor Island

Seal Island

Tongue Point

13

Tongue Neck

Mott Island

Grassy Island

Russian Island

Minaker Island

Tongue Point Village

East Mooring Basin Boat Launch

Lois Island

7

Navy Heights

30

30

Cathlamet Bay

Settler Point

Svensen Island

oria

Mill Creek Road

John Day County Park Boat

CSF

Fern Hill

South Channel

Svensen

CLATSOP STATE FOREST

John Day

River

CSF

Svensen Junction

30

202

Wicks Road

CSF

Youngs River

CSF

Pipeline Road

Bear Creek

6

2. THE RED LINE

A string of red channel markers, starting from Buoy 10 and extending through buoy numbers 12, 14, 20 and 22, are most often fished on the incoming tide using a combination of back-trolling techniques and holding steadfast in the current.

Baker Bay

If the number 10 buoy isn't calling your name at low slack, then head over to the Washington side and back-troll the area in front of the Ilwaco wing dams and Baker Bay pilings. This area tends to hold a lot of baitfish. Back-troll all the way through the Sand Island slot, at mid-tide forward troll toward Chinook.

3. SAND ISLAND TROLL

The pilings in this area create tidal rips that tend to hold a lot of baitfish, and the troll fishes well on both incoming and outgoing tides. If you have back-trolled from Buoy 10 through Buoy 14, you can cut across to the Washington side and continue back-trolling or forward trolling upriver using a diver-and-bait or a diver-and-herring rig between 8 and 20 pulls. From here you can continue to forward troll on the incoming mid-tide through the beginning of Church Hole and on upriver past the Astoria-Megler Bridge.

This area also fishes excellently on an outgoing tide from the Chinook entrance to the river with a downstream troll using a cannonball/spreader-bar setup with a large Fish Flash flasher leading to a spinner or herring. Be cautious of all the pilings at Baker Bay; there are tons of them. Your baits should be near the bottom on the outgoing tide here, and you should troll downstream through breakwater piling numbers 5, 3 and then finally number 1 before picking up your gear and making another pass.

4. HAMMOND

At the halfway point of the flood tide, boats will start holding against the current in front of the Hammond entrance in the main shipping channel. If you leapfrogged to Hammond earlier, then wait for the fish to come to you. Again, a diver-and-bait or a diver-and-spinner setup works excellently in this area.

Here you can back-troll up to Warrenton, then pick your gear up and make one or more passes.

5. THE SAWDUST PILE

This hole is located at the Warrenton Fiber Nygaard Logging Company. There may be more than a few large piles of sawdust here that can be easily seen from the river, or you may just see a few logging barges. The Sawdust Pile is downriver from the Warrenton boat ramp and the entrance to Skipanon Waterway.

This is a great place for anglers launching out of Warrenton to start their day. Lots of limits are filled right in front of the river.

If you've started your voyage from the number 10 buoy at the crack of dawn at low slack, then you've arrived here just in time for a savage take-down. This i the perfect mid-tide spot to just point your bow toward the ocean and hold your boat in the current.

It's also a great back-trolling area to let your boat slip upriver toward the beginning of the Green Line. If there were nets in the air on your first pass and you didn't get bit, then pick up your gear and back-troll or forward troll into the Green Line once again.

6. THE GREEN LINE

The namesake for this troll is a long line of green buoys numbered 25 through 29 which straddle the south channel.

The Green Line fishes well on an incoming tide while holding your boat in the current, back-trolling upriver, or forward trolling in the south channel toward the Astoria-Megler Bridge. On an incoming tide you can run your divers a few pulls deeper here, 15 to 30 pulls, but this area also fishes excellently on a downstream troll on an outgoing tide. You will want your cannonball/spreader-rigs hugging the bottom in 30 to 40 feet of water.

Make sure to stay on the north side of these buoys which mark the dividing line to the Young's Bay Control Zone. At this time, Young's bay is off limits, but wait for future announcements in case this fishery is opened again.

The Green Line is the perfect place to intercept Young's Bay Select Area Bright (SAB) Chinook that originally came from the Rogue River and are marked with a left ventral fin clip. These SABs are esteemed food fish and formidable fighters.

As the incoming tide starts to weaken you can set your divers a few more pulls out or you can switch over to cannonball/spreader-bar rigs and troll right up the south channel alongside Desdemona Sands under the Astoria-Megler Bridge and further up into downtown Astoria.

7. DOWNTOWN ASTORIA

On the outgoing tide, trolling in the south channel (the main shipping channel) starting just upriver from the Astoria-Megler Bridge near the East Boat Basin and performing a downstream troll while entering the Green Line is excellent. Make sure that your cannonball sinker is bumping bottom on occasion in 25 to 30 feet of water. This is really great spinner water

The Tunnel

This is a well-known landmark for getting your bearings. Located just downriver from Church Hole closer to the town of Chinook, a tunnel can often be seen with cars passing through it.

8. CHURCH HOLE

As of 2015 the church spire for which this troll was named could still be easily seen from the river. This troll is productive on both incoming and outgoing tides for mostly Chinook, and it produces well on both soft and wide tidal exchanges. Maps and charts often identify the church by the word "spire", which is about midway through the troll.

Some people say that this particular spot stops and starts right at the Astoria-Megler Bridge, but Church Hole really starts upriver from the bridge in deep water and extends west near the entrance to the Chinook boat basin. The average depth is between 30 and 40 feet, but there are some really deep holes just upriver and downriver from the bridge that average 50 feet or more and get lots of angler attention. During warm-water conditions, chinook will duck into these cooler, deeper holes where anglers can pick them off by using heavy cannonball sinkers with spinners, whole herring or cut-plug herring.

A lot of anglers will work the 25- to 35-foot edges for coho, especially the ridges along the edge of Desdemona Sands. Church Hole can be fished on both the ebb and flood tides and is one of the most forgiving spots as far as techniques go. Church Hole is one of the most popular spots on the river.

9. THE BLIND CHANNEL

This is by far my favorite trolling spot when there is a soft tide exchange occurring during high slack, as well as for the entire outgoing tide cycle. I've caught upriver brights here on the turn of low tide and on the incoming tide as well. It fishes superbly on both the incoming and outgoing tides. But it is also one of the best pieces of water to fish during slack-water periods because chinook will often hold here at the turn of high tide after they have hitched a ride on the tide from Buoy 10 through the entire flood cycle.

The Blind Channel straddles water that can range from 25 to 50 feet deep, but it has a well-deserved name. You can be in 30 feet of water one second and 5 feet the next. Tilt-shift sonar, which allows you to see these upcoming high spots before they are upon you, is a plus in this area.

The deeper spots transition into Church Hole but The Blind Channel also transitions into Shipwreck Troll as well. Cannonball/spreader-bar setups with sinkers ranging from 10 to 16 ounces work well here, especially on the outgoing and slack tides, but are

superior fishing methods on the incoming tide as well.

You can fish for suspended fish in the deeper sections but I prefer to be right on the bottom, following the 40- to 50-foot contours by watching my fish finder. Cut-plug herring works really well here, as do spinners. You might want to put a Dick's Sure Spin rotating helmet on your cut-plug herring, or a Bechhold Rotary Bullet Bait Holder on your whole herring and anchovies, with both helmets sporting the color chartreuse.

This area has two distinct separations of water where you will see two different trolling lines. One is closer to shore while the other is further out in the estuary. A definite must-troll area if you've never fished the Buoy 10 arena.

10. MILLION DOLLAR OUTHOUSE

Straddling the upper end of Church Hole which extends upriver from the Astoria-Megler Bridge is a rest area with restroom facilities that can be easily spotted from the bank. You will often see a hundred or more boats trolling this area on either an incoming or outgoing tide.

11. SHIPWRECK TROLL

In a small cove extending further upriver from Million Dollar Outhouse, you can see an old ship that ran aground with its mast pointing toward the river. A little bit further upriver you will also see an old rusty barge. Stick to the 30-foot line whenever possible in this very productive troll that produces on both the incoming and outgoing tides.

I've also often seen boats fishing even closer to shore here, usually locals in smaller vessels. They do quite well using the same rigs as discussed before but there aren't nearly as many hookups as in the deeper water.

Day Marker; aka the Checkerboard

Many years ago there used to be a yellow buoy that marked the western-most edge of the very dangerous shoal, Desdemona Sands. Now there is a 3-legged black-and-white sign (hence the name). The ever-changing sands of Desdemona could at any time extend further downriver from the Day Marker on any given year, so exercise extra caution around this place.

That being said, holding here on an incoming tide is the go-to technique.

12. DESDEMONA SANDS

This constantly-changing shoal is approximately 8 miles long, with 2/3 of it being on the downriver side of the Astoria-Megler Bridge and about 1/3 of it extending above the bridge. To appreciate the menacing prominence of this island, everyone

should look at it while traveling between states on the Astoria-Megler Bridge. From this height, the shape of Desdemona sticks out like a sore thumb, especially during low tide.

Strong incoming and outgoing ocean currents, in addition to high river flows, form the north and south channels adjacent to Desdemona Sands. And there is no doubt that the enormous cement pilings that hold up the bridge played an integral part in forming the channels as well. Both channels fish extremely well.

Be very aware of your boat's height when going under the bridge, many boats have had their crow's nests, radar and antennae ripped off their vessels. When you are trolling alongside hundreds of other boats, there is usually not enough room to spin your boat around the other way as everyone will be trolling in the same direction and in very close quarters.

North and South Channel

If you have your sights set on chinook, your best bet any day during August would be to troll in the North and South Channel adjacent to Desdemona Sands; the coho fishing can be off the charts at times as well. Of note, both North and South Channels are a chinook's first resting spot, where they stage for several days before committing themselves to their upriver journeys. During a soft tide exchange, they can stage as long as one week.

For chinook on an outgoing tide make sure that you are on the bottom and work every bottom contour that you can. Heavy cannonball sinkers ranging between 10 and 16 ounces will assure that your rig stays down on the bottom and creates fewer chances of snagging other anglers' lines.

Incoming tides produce well using a diver-and-bait

A lot of people from around the Northwest look forward to the Buoy 10 fishery each season. For some, it is the event of the year. Here, two boats use the Buoy as a marker, waiting for the bite to start.

or diver-and-spinner setup. Make sure that you snap a big triangular-style flasher, like a Fish Flash or a Kone Zone flasher, directly to the end of the diver. Leaders will range from 5 to 8 feet, depending on the size of your rod.

The North Channel is a false channel because it dead-ends from deep water to shallow water while rolling downriver toward Ilwaco. The lead edge of the flood tide tends to push fish into the North Channel, especially off of Baker Bay, which attracts both chinook and coho into the Sand Island Troll, where you can clobber them by performing a downstream roll.

The South Channel is a great place to fish but it is also the shipping channel. Those big freighters coming into port always have the right of way, so if you see one of them coming your way make sure to give it plenty of room. They couldn't stop if they wanted to. If you get too close to an incoming freighter, the U.S. Coast Guard can and will issue you a very expensive ticket. You will also want to be extremely wary of cutting in back of large tugs boats. Remember that a tug boat's purpose is to tow things, like large barges. If a tug happens to be towing a barge, the barge will not make a sound because it will not be under power. If you cut across the back of a tug towing a barge, it can cost you your life.

13. TONGUE POINT

This is the second staging area for chinook and coho and is the go-to spot after the Buoy 10 fishery closes. Chinook and coho are both caught here using a variety of trolling methods. Some fish will be coming back to the SAFE-area fisheries, so when the season is open be sure to stay west of the upriver boundary. SAFE stands for Select Area Fisheries and there are four of them (see attachment) where additional fall chinook and coho are raised for the Columbia River. The SAFE program is now being run by Clatsop County Fisheries. The number of salmon raised varies every year. The SAFE-area fisheries provide extra fishing opportunity the Buoy 10 fishery, in addition to the regular WDFW, ODFW and tribal entities that supply salmon to the fishery.

After the Buoy 10 fishery closes it's game on trolling for chinook and coho in the area from Tongue to Rice Island.

When the bite is hot here you can launch at the John Day boat ramp and be here in 5 minutes, or launch at Lori's Launch on Deep River and make it here in 10 minutes. The East Mooring Basin is only a few miles west of Tongue Point. This area produces best on an incoming tide.

In conclusion, those are the 18 best places to fish in the Buoy 10 fishery, with the most noted trolls and most popular fishing spots included. This information should provide enough ammunition for you to hook up with some strapping chinook and scrappy coho somewhere in the Buoy 10 fishery.

Photo by Gary Lewis

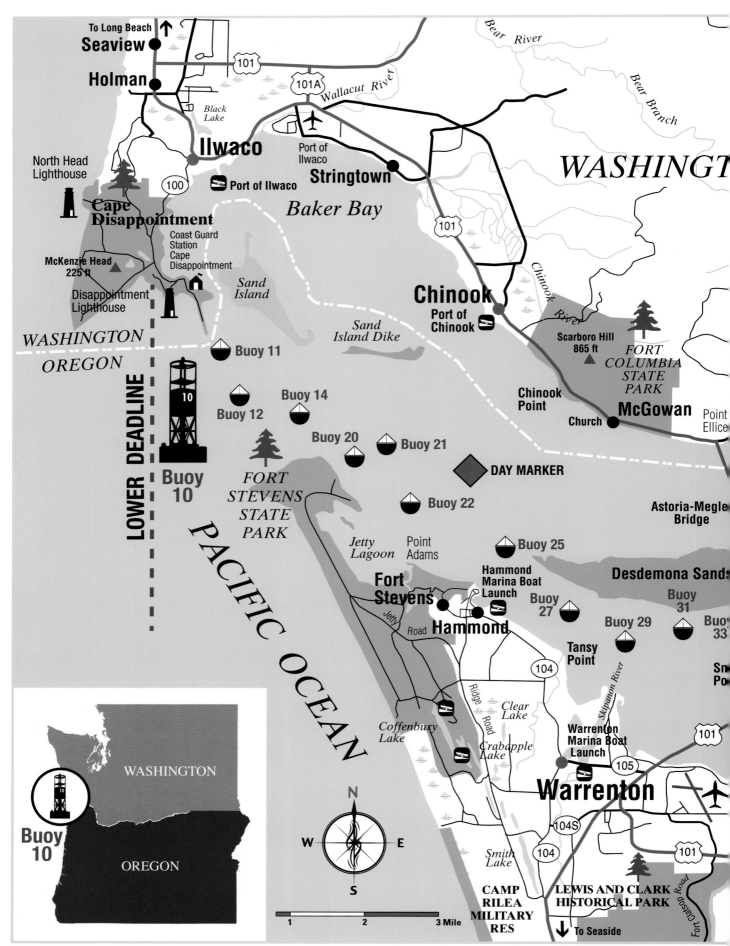

To Long Beach

Seaview

Holman

Bear River

Bear Branch

101

101A

Wallacut River

Black Lake

Ilwaco

Port of Ilwaco

Stringtown

WASHINGTON

North Head Lighthouse

Cape Disappointment

Port of Ilwaco

Baker Bay

101

McKenzie Head 225 ft

Coast Guard Station Cape Disappointment

Disappointment Lighthouse

Sand Island

Chinook

Port of Chinook

Chinook River

Scarboro Hill 865 ft

FORT COLUMBIA STATE PARK

WASHINGTON

OREGON

Sand Island Dike

Chinook Point

McGowan

Point Ellice

Buoy 11

Church

Buoy 14

Buoy 12

LOWER DEADLINE

Buoy 10

10

FORT STEVENS STATE PARK

Buoy 20

Buoy 21

DAY MARKER

Astoria-Megle Bridge

Buoy 22

Buoy 25

Desdemona Sands

PACIFIC OCEAN

Jetty Lagoon

Point Adams

Hammond Marina Boat Launch

Buoy 27

Buoy 31

Buoy 29

Buoy 33

Fort Stevens

Hammond

Jetty Road

Tansy Point

104

Sn Po

Ridge Road

Clear Lake

Warrenton Marina Boat Launch

101

Coffenbury Lake

Crabapple Lake

105

N

WASHINGTON

Buoy 10

OREGON

W   E

S

Smith Lake

Warrenton

104S

104

101

CAMP RILEA MILITARY RES

LEWIS AND CLARK HISTORICAL PARK

To Seaside

Fort Clatsop Road

1   2   3 Mile

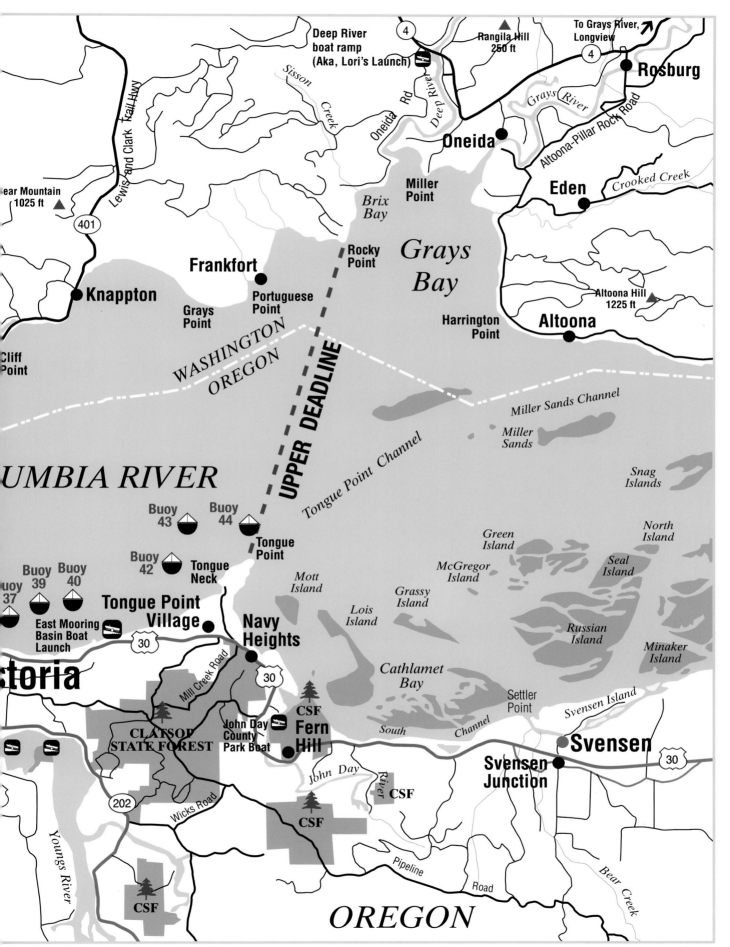

Deep River boat ramp
(Aka, Lori's Launch)

4

Rangila Hill
250 ft

To Grays River,
Longview

4

Rosburg

Grays River

Sisson Creek

Oneida Rd

Deep River

Altoona-Pillar Rock Road

Oneida

Miller
Point

Eden

Crooked Creek

ear Mountain
1025 ft

Lewis and Clark Trail Hwy

*Brix
Bay*

401

Rocky
Point

*Grays
Bay*

Frankfort

Altoona Hill
1225 ft

Knappton

Portuguese
Point

Grays
Point

Altoona

Harrington
Point

Cliff
Point

WASHINGTON

OREGON

Miller Sands Channel

*Miller
Sands*

UMBIA RIVER

*Snag
Islands*

Tongue Point Channel

UPPER DEADLINE

Buoy
43

Buoy
44

*North
Island*

*Green
Island*

Buoy
42

Tongue
Neck

Tongue
Point

*McGregor
Island*

*Seal
Island*

Buoy
39

Buoy
40

Mott
Island

*Grassy
Island*

*Russian
Island*

Buoy
37

East Mooring
Basin Boat
Launch

**Tongue Point
Village**

**Navy
Heights**

*Lois
Island*

*Minaker
Island*

storia

30

30

*Cathlamet
Bay*

Settler
Point

Svensen Island

Svensen

Mill Creek Road

CSF

**Fern
Hill**

**CLATSOP
STATE FOREST**

John Day
County
Park Boat

South

Channel

**Svensen
Junction**

30

202

John Day River

CSF

Wicks Road

CSF

Youngs River

Pipeline

Road

Bear Creek

CSF

OREGON

Chapter 12

Buoy 10

Keep Your...

B-B-B-Bait
C-C-C-Cold

After salting down the ice, burrow an inexpensive plastic container into the ice mixture which will hold all your anchovy and herring trays and keep them in a near-freezing state. Placing some fresh baitfish in the bottom of the container will allow the baitfish to freeze so you can plug-cut them later.

t never ceases to amaze me that fishermen will not think twice about spending $30,000.00 for a brand-new boat, $600.00 for a new rod and reel, and $500.00 for a 2-night stay at a good motel, yet they will skimp on the most important item — bait!

I cannot stress enough the importance of caring for your bait by keeping your herring or anchovies cold. And when I say cold, I'm talking nearly frozen; the consistency of a Popsicle is the perfect texture. Caring for your bait properly is essential for maximizing your strike potential.

There are various reasons to keep your baitfish this cold, whether you intend on using frozen or fresh herring, anchovies or sardines.

First of all, it is a lot easier to thread hooks through a semi-frozen bait than a soft mushy bait.

Second, and most important, don't let your bait thaw to room temperature. As soon as that happens, bacteria starts to grow and it's game over for salmon bites.

A salmon's life depends on its sense of smell till its last dying breath. Its sense of smell guides it from the ocean back to its original birth water which might be thousands of miles from where it grew to mammoth proportions in the Gulf of Alaska.

Salmon smell in parts per billion whereas other fish "only" smell in parts per million (or less), and can smell a bait that has gone bad long before it has ever come near it. They can sniff things out better than a dog, so you don't want to offend a salmon before it has even had the chance to see your bait.

The way to keep your baitfish cold is to have a separate cooler dedicated solely for bait. Put several layers of ice on the bottom and spread non-iodized table salt on top of the ice. This turns your cooler into a freezer. Your bait will remain frozen for a very long time, and will thaw to the consistency of a Popsicle. It will remain that way as long as you keep putting more ice and salt into the cooler. If you are buying fresh herring at the dock, get the bait on top of this ice/salt mixture as soon as possible.

You also need a separate tray that sits just over the ice (plastic food containers and lids make perfect trays) to put the baitfish into. Many ice chests come equipped with built-in trays; take the time to look for this type of ice chest — it is time well spent.

I prefer to use frozen herring or anchovies because they are starved while they are live in the net pens. This causes the fishes' stomachs and intestines to shrink, and all of the contents inside their stomachs are used up. Frozen baits also tend to retain all their scales. Every scale on a frozen bait is like an individual lure that throws out an alluring flash.

Fresh herring is available at most docks in the morning, and must be ordered the night before your trip. Fresh baitfish are great because they were just killed that morning, but they are only good if they were kept cold. There's nothing that matches the beautiful iridescent sheen on the sides of a freshly-killed herring. Because they are fresh, they do tend to lose their scales. They also haven't been starved so their guts are very full. But if you put them on your ice/salt mixture right away, they will become semi-frozen in about 20 minutes. If you are going to plug-cut them, it really won't matter that they haven't been starved since you will be removing their guts after you make the first cut anyway.

Keeping your bait ice-cold will keep your bait from spoiling and you will get more hookups because of it. At the end of the day, wash out your cooler with water and Lemon Joy, which is the staple for fishermen in the Pacific Northwest when it comes to cleaning plugs and ice chests.

STRAIGHT WHOLE BAITFISH OR NOSE CONES?

When fishing a whole herring or anchovy, I use some type of head helmet which are designed to put a spin on the bait. If your bait is not spinning while you are trolling, you are wasting your time.

A lot of people get ribbed about using these things, for not being able to spin their own baitfish. But I can put any spin I want on my baitfish and I still prefer using nose cones — they work that well!

There are several good ones on the market. The FBR made by Shelton Products is exceptional, as is the Rotary Salmon Killer made by Pro-Troll. But I can tell you with confidence that the Bechhold Rotary Bullet Bait holder is the best on the market. I've caught a lot of Buoy 10 chinook on this puppy. This particular helmet can be used with an anchovy or a herring. It has low-profile fins, which I believe are a big advantage because a salmon's mouth doesn't feel them as easily as the other brands that have sharply-pointed, more-protruding fins. Whichever model you choose to use, all colors will work as long as they are chartreuse.

I expect more companies will be releasing nose cones in the near future.

CUT-PLUG HERRING

Cut-plug herring are one of the deadliest baits in the Buoy 10 fishery. This is one bait you can put a wicked spin on without an artificial spinning device.

When plug-cutting my own herring, I buy blue-label size herring or the larger purple-label size, or I buy fresh bait that is large enough to plug-cut. Fresh bait works extremely well as cut-plug herring because you are keeping them nearly frozen in your specially-made bait freezer.

Fresh cut-plug herring are a lot sturdier than you might think because the main hook is inserted through the baitfish's spine. This way you can troll with one bait over an extended period of time before it finally falls apart — often in the inside of a salmon's mouth.

There is a lot of talk about whether or not to brine your baits. My opinion is that brined baits take away from the fish's natural scent, however I do make an exception when it comes to cut-plug herring. Brining cut-plug herring is common in this fishery. People brine their cut-plugs so that they remain a little tougher and troll for a longer period of time without getting ripped up. If you decide to go this route, make sure you follow the directions for freezing them in your cooler. A brined herring at room temperature may spin well, but it will still offend a salmon long before the fish comes within eyeshot of the bait. Keep your brined herring as cold as the rest of your bait.

If you want to brine your baits, keep it simple. Never use bottled water as it may contain offensive minerals or even chlorine which will turn off a salmon very quickly. Don't brine your baits in tap water either because it has had chemicals added at some point.

If you do decide to brine your own bait, use river water — the exact stuff that the fish will be swimming through on their Buoy 10 journey. I use one cup of rock salt to one quart of river water and call it good. And again, make sure that you keep it very cold.

There are some good commercial brines on the market. I have done quite well using Pautzke's Fire Brine in the color chartreuse. This stuff comes ready to use: just pour it over your baitfish in a plastic container and put the covered container in the refrigerator the night before your trip.

If you do decide to go the helmet route, Dick's Sure Spin makes an excellent helmet for putting a nice spin on a cut-plug herring.

However you prepare your cut-plug herring, make sure that you keep your bait very, very cold and you will definitely be ahead of the hook-up game at Buoy 10.

Devon Pearsall with a boat's limit of silver salmon, most of which came during a frenzied half hour of fishing. At one moment the anglers had three fish on at once.

Spreading a liberal amount of non-iodized salt on your ice chest's ice for every 4 inches of vertical height will quickly turn your ice chest into a freezer, critical for keeping your baitfish ice cold.

Chapter 13

Buoy 10

The Power Setups of...

Buoy 10

With the wall-to-wall gunwale scenario at today's Buoy 10 fishery, anglers need to get their fish into the boat as quickly as they can to avoid tangling other anglers' lines.

This new modus operandi has changed the way that people rig-up. I call these new setups 'power rigs'. They are basically souped-up setups of yesteryear with a few novel twists.

In addition to the fishery being quite crowded, you are only allowed to use barbless hooks in this fishery. If your hook doesn't come barbless, you must pinch the barb off with a pair of needlenose pliers. Actually it was the barbless-hook ruling that had more of an effect on the way people fish Buoy 10 today than anything else.

Before the mega-huge crowds came along, and when you were allowed to use barbed hooks, you could play a fish and let it make all the runs that it desired before you finally brought the tired salmon to the net.

With this fishery now being so crowded, compounded with a barbless-only hook regulation, anglers have been forced to upsize their main line and leader diameters, increase their hook sizes and tighten down their drags. In fact, your drag should be cranked down so tight that you can barely pull the line off of your reel by hand. Most people will not be able to pull line off the reel at all.

You will soon realize why these fish have earned the title of king when you have a drag that is set so tight you are forced to go one-on-one with the raw power of these dynamic fighters. All I can say is that you better be holding onto your rod with all your might. Some people might call this 'horsing them in' and, to a certain degree, that is exactly what the fishery has evolved into. But that doesn't mean that it isn't fun; in fact it's a blast! Two things that you will never be short of at Buoy 10 is a racing heart and lots of adrenaline rushes.

There is a positive way of looking at getting the fish in faster. With the barbless-hook restriction, I believe that by using more power to get these fish to the net, the landing ratio has been higher, much like what it is in the commercial salmon industry.

Having a fish on for a shorter period of time will protect the inside of a salmon's mouth. When you fight a fish for a long time, the constant pressure causes rips and tears in the inside of a salmon's mouth, which is one of the reasons why many salmon are lost. That's not going to happen when you have your drag wrenched down tightly. If you do lose a fish, you are going to lose it right off the bat. Most of the time it will stay hooked and come to the net as long as you don't give it any slack.

Of course I loved the fishery when hooks had barbs on them. That was your insurance in case you accidentally dipped your rod tip too low or your line went slack for whatever reason. But those days are gone now.

BEEF-UP YOUR GEAR

Start your rigging by loading your reels with 65-pound braided line for your main line. Examples of great lines are Power Pro or Tracer Braid.

For a stalwart salmon reel, you can't go wrong with an Ambassadeur 6500, either one that has a line counter or the standard model. However any good conventional reel with an excellent drag system will do the job. There are lots of Shimano, Daiwa and Penn reels being used in this fishery.

Check your drags at least six weeks in advance of your trip and replace worn drag washers or have a reputable reel repair service do it for you. I have grown especially partial to the Smooth Drag Company which makes all those great carbon-fiber drag washers for every reel known to man.

You will also want to start running at least 40-pound monofilament leaders, such as Berkley Big Game or Maxima Ultragreen. And a lot of folks are starting to use 50-pound leaders for insurance purposes. These fish are not leader shy.

Another thing that has changed the face of the Buoy 10 fishery is that long rods are starting to become the industry standard, and when I mean long, I'm talking about rods that are at least 10 1/2 feet long. Both Lamiglas and Berkley make rods that cater to this fishery. The go-to Lamiglas rod is the XCC 1064 GH, while the Berkley equivalent is the A92-10-6HH.

Why use a 10 1/2-foot rod, you might ask? Because a lot of people are now using leaders as long as 8 feet. If you use an 8-foot rod with an 8-foot leader, by the time you factor in the length of the diver and flasher with all of the jewelry attached, and take into consideration that there will be a considerable bend to the rod, you would never land the fish. You might get to see the fish if you're lucky, but that's about it. Been there, done that. Not doing it again. I'll go with 10 1/2-footers any day of the year.

Another reason to use a long rod is because it the rod acts like a shock absorber. It tends to stay loaded up even if you accidently take a step forward or if the water is a little on the rough side. In a barbless-hook fishery, fish are lost as soon as the rod goes limp. Long rods are very forgiving and tend to maintain a certain amount of bend most of the time, thereby always maintaining just enough pressure on the fish to keep the hooks buried inside its mouth.

HOW A SALMON EATS A TROLLED BAITFISH AKA, THE WAITING GAME

Long rods will also help you get more hookups because of the way salmon are forced to eat your bait. When a salmon munches down on a herring in the wild, it inhales the bait inside its mouth head-first and then swallows it in one big gulp. That process only takes a split second. But when they are trying to munch on a trolled herring they cannot eat the baitfish in the same manner because its head is being pulled by stiff monofilament. That stiff line in the front of the herring feels very strange to a salmon.

When a salmon eats a trolled herring the sensitive nerve endings in its mouth feel that something is not quite right. The salmon is forced to turn the baitfish around in its mouth in order to swallow it — and that takes time! What took only a split second to do in the wild, now takes up to 30 seconds or more to do in a trolled situation, and knowing this will help you get more hookups, in addition to teaching you a little patience in not being too quick on the stick.

If the salmon feels anything out of the ordinary as far as pressure in its mouth goes, it will spit out your bait. That's why most guides prefer that their clients not hold their fishing rods, because the knee-jerk reaction when a person feels a nibble is to immediately yank back on the rod as hard as they can. If you do this, what I call a hay-baling hook-set during the beginning to mid-stages when a salmon starts turning the bait around in its mouth, your chances of hooking this fish are slim to none.

Watching how a salmon eats your baitfish is a thrill to behold, and in the process you will gain a whole new level of appreciation for good-quality fishing rods. Imagine that a salmon sees a nice-looking herring being trolled at a consistent rate of speed. The salmon's first reaction is to follow the bait at the speed the boat is traveling. It will savor the fish in its mouth while it is swimming, and suck the bait into its mouth while traveling at the speed of your boat. On your rod tip, that first step is usually indicated by a slight bounce of your rod, a slight bend, or your rod might just quickly bounce down and then up one time. The salmon's sensitive nerve endings sense that there is something strange about the baitfish that will prevent the salmon from gulping it down in the ordinary way, so it just keeps swimming at the same speed of your boat. Sometimes nothing happens for a second or more. But be patient. The name of the game is 'WAIT If you jerk now, it's game over. You will never see that fish again.

Once the salmon realizes that it will not be able to swallow the baitfish head-first in one gulp, it will try to turn the baitfish around in its mouth. As it is doing this, your rod might do any number of things. It might get a deeper bend or it could dip down and up several times in rapid succession while the rod is bent. The temptation to yard back on your rod at this time starts to dominate your thinking, but you must have the patience to leave your rod in its holder or else you will surely lose the fish.

When the salmon has almost completely turned the bait around in its mouth, your rod gets an even deeper bend, while bobbing up and down at the same time. Resist the temptation to touch your rod. As the saying goes, "All good things to those who wait." When the salmon finally turns the baitfish around in its mouth and makes the commitment to swallow it, the salmon will usually make some kind of turn. This swallowing process might take anywhere from 5 seconds up to 30 seconds or more.

At this point your rod tip will meet the surface of the water and line will be screaming off of your reel. You can now carefully slide the rod out of its rod holder and you're off to the races with a salmon that's gone berserk. You do not need to set the hook because at this point the fish has done the hook-setting for you. When it takes out line against 34 pounds of pressure from your drag, rest assured that the hook has been set. In fact if you set the hook now, you could very easily lose the fish. It will probably make one or two 15 yard runs, if that, but it will not be making the 50-yard runs of yesteryear when you could use a loose drag.

This is why rod holders are so important in this fishery. You get to see every bite in the herring-eating process and, for me, watching the bite is just as exciting as fighting the fish. You can really see it when using 10-1/2-foot rods because the rod has enough bend that the salmon doesn't really feel any pressure inside its mouth until it is too late.

In summary, using a long rod is insurance for getting those first-biting salmon to stick around for the second course, which is turning the baitfish around in its mouth. The shock-absorbing qualities of a long rod enable the salmon to munch on your bait for longer periods of time before it finally decides to swallow it. The salmon doesn't feel as much resistance on the baitfish as it dines on your herring, consequently you will get more hookups. As a result of using longer rods, your baitfish is often found deeper down the fish's throat after you land it.

WHAT TO USE AND WHEN

For fishing the western-most end of the fishery on an incoming tide I like to use a diver-and-bait or diver-and-spinner setup. These rigs work quite well on the incoming tide at Buoy 10 as well as up toward the Astoria-Megler Bridge during mid-tide or even during the outgoing tide. But a lot of anglers are now using heavy cannonball/wire spreader rigs to get their gear down on the last half of an incoming tide or for the entire outgoing tide series.

When fishing with heavy sinkers on an outgoing tide you will want to be as close to the bottom as possible for chinook, working the dishes and the bottom contour. From time to time, I will lift up my rod a few feet and let the rig fall back to the bottom. If I do not feel the cannonball sinker touching bottom, I will let out line until I feel the sinker banging the bottom. If you are not within six feet of the bottom on an outgoing tide, you are in for a very long day.

I like to look at my fish finder as well when fishing this fishery so I can see exactly where the fish are and how deep I need to place my bait. Sometimes during high or low slack, the fish will suspend, in which case it is OK to bring your bait further up toward the surface. But most of the time on an outgoing tide you will need to feel your sinker occasionally touching bottom in order to be in the bite zone.

I disable the 'Fish I.D.' feature on my fish finder to judge for myself if that big arch on the screen is a fish, an underwater log or a big clump of grass. Often, the 'Fish I.D.' feature misidentifies free-floating moss, air bubbles or other debris in the water as fish.

DIVER AND BAIT

The diver-and-bait setup is one of the most effective rigs in this fishery. The two most effective divers are the Double Deep Six Divers made by Luhr Jensen and the Delta Diver. Just as the name implies, they dive down in the water column and present your flasher and bait to salmon that are at various depths in the water column. Both diver brands are made in different colors to attract salmon. The Double Deep Six is available in chartreuse crystal, pink crystal and silver and is also available with comet tails. Comet tails are ornamental silver-stranded tassels that hang off of each side of the diver. Sometimes more flash in the water equates to hotter fishing.

One of my favorite rigs is what I call 'The Ultimate Red Setup for Coho and Chinook.' Coho are known to go for colors like shocking pink and bright red, and chinook like them as well. This rig utilizes a Pink Crystal Double Deep Six Diver with comet tails, a red Fish Flash flasher, a red Salmon Bungee and a large number 6 1/2 Toman Thumper Flex Squid Spinner in Luminous Fluorescent Red. It also has a hot pink-colored squid tail on it as well. I keep at least two of these rigs on hand. This rig will be explained in more detail when the topic 'Salmon Bungees' is addressed later in this chapter.

Delta Divers offer a wider variety of holographic colors, including chartreuse, dark red, dark green and silver just to name a few. One advantage of these different colors is that you can match the color of the diver to the color of your flasher, or get pretty darned close. Since the Delta Diver is flat, you can actually buy colored tape to match your flasher and apply the tape on the diver yourself.

The Double Deep Six Diver uses two keel weights to help it dive deeper, as opposed to the regular Deep Six Diver which has only one keel weight attached. The standard Deep Six Diver will work in this fishery, but most fishermen like to use the Double Deep Six Diver because it will dive deeper at a faster rate and allow you to fish closer to the boat, thereby avoiding tangles with other boats.

Like all Deep Six Divers, the Double Deep Six utilizes a screw-tightening release mechanism that allows the diver to trip when a fish has eaten the bait or lure, or you can trip the mechanism yourself by giving the rod a hard yank in order to bring the diver back to the boat without feeling any resistance from the diver. You can adjust the release-tightening screw with an ordinary screwdriver if it is releasing too easily or is not tripping when it should.

The Delta Diver does not actually trip like the Double Deep Six Diver, but when a fish eats the bait or lure, a barrel swivel at the back of the diver positions itself so that you will not feel any resistance from the diver while fighting the fish. But for the most part, the Delta Diver will always keep your rod bent unless you are hooked-up with a strapping salmon.

I have caught salmon on both diver brands, but I prefer using the Delta Diver in the 4-ounce model which is their largest and heaviest diver. I believe that the Delta Diver has the capacity for diving deeper, faster and steeper than any other diver. I know from my ocean salmon trips that this diver will dive to 75 feet with ease. Luhr Jensen claims that the Double Deep Six 002 model will dive to 135 feet, and that may be true, but I will still stick to the Delta Brand which I believe runs truer. But I will always carry both brands with me when I go fishing.

RIGGING-UP A DIVER

Rigging-up a diver is a breeze. Start out by tying 65-pound braid main line directly to a corkscrew swivel. These swivels are the only way to go for quick-changing rigs. Once you have used corkscrew swivels, you will wonder what took you so long. Use a high-quality swivel made in the USA; Englund Marine sells the good stuff because they cater to commercial fishermen.

Attach the diver of your choice to the corkscrew swivel. The next step will require just a little retrofitting on the welded rings at both ends of the Fish Flash.

What makes Fish Flash flashers spin so well is the fact that high-quality ball-bearing swivels are attached to each end of the flasher, with the turning ends of the ball-bearing swivels facing the flasher. On the end of each ball-bearing swivel is a welded ring. Using your split-ring pliers, attach a high-quality split ring to the welded ring at each end of the flasher. On the rear of the Fish Flash attach a 6-bead bead-chain swivel to the split ring.

At the front of the Fish Flash, attach just the eyelet end of a corkscrew snap to that split ring. If you cannot get a corkscrew snap without a barrel swivel attached, cut off the barrel swivel with a pair of wire cutters. Now you can attach the Fish Flash directly to the back of the diver of your choice using the corkscrew swivel at the front of the flasher.

SPINNERS

Spinners are very popular in the Buoy 10 fishery and

RETRO-FITTED FISH FLASH

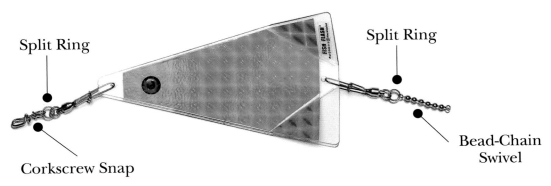

Split Ring

Split Ring

Corkscrew Snap

Bead-Chain Swivel

When your Delta Diver is rigged-up to a Fish Flash flasher, you can use a spinner, a cut-plug herring, or a whole herring inside of a nose cone at the end of your leader.

Delta Diver

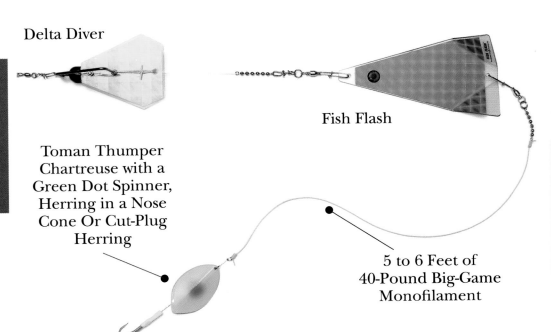

Toman Thumper Chartreuse with a Green Dot Spinner, Herring in a Nose Cone Or Cut-Plug Herring

Fish Flash

5 to 6 Feet of 40-Pound Big-Game Monofilament

hey work from the Buoy 10 deadline to Tongue Point. Anglers use big spinner blades in this fishery, with sizes 6, 6 1/2 and 7 being common, but the most frequently-used size blade is a 6 1/2.

You can have a field day choosing spinner blade colors but the diagonal red-and-white spinner is the classic Buoy 10 special. Chartreuse with a green dot and green with a chartreuse tip are other popular colors. You never know what color is going to work the best from year to year, so don't get locked in to using what worked last year, although that particular spinner might be the go-to color this year as well.

Running spinners from the back of the aforementioned diver/flasher rig is quite common in this fishery. To rig-up, simply tie a 5- or 6-foot leader of 40-pound monofilament to the eyelet running from bead chain in the back of your retrofitted Fish Flash, and then tie the other end of the leader to the spinner of your choice, which in this case might be a size 6 1/2, red and white Toman's Thumper Flex Squid Spinner.

From here you can start forward trolling, back-trolling or holding in the current.

These big spinners usually come equipped with very large and strong hooks that will hold most fish with the drag screwed down tightly. But some folks feel that they have a better hookup and landing ratio by using a single hook on the back end. If you decide to go this route, cut off the treble hook and replace it with a 4/0 owner Siwash hook.

If you had a choice of only two spinners to carry in your tackle box, I would carry a size 6-1/2 Toman spinner in either the color red-and-white with a pink squid tail or what is called chartreuse/green dot with a chartreuse squid tail.

HERRING OR ANCHOVIES

If you want to run a whole herring or anchovy, I heartily recommend running it inside of a nose cone of some sort. Tie or purchase a 2-hook sliding mooching leader and use a 5- or 6-foot piece of

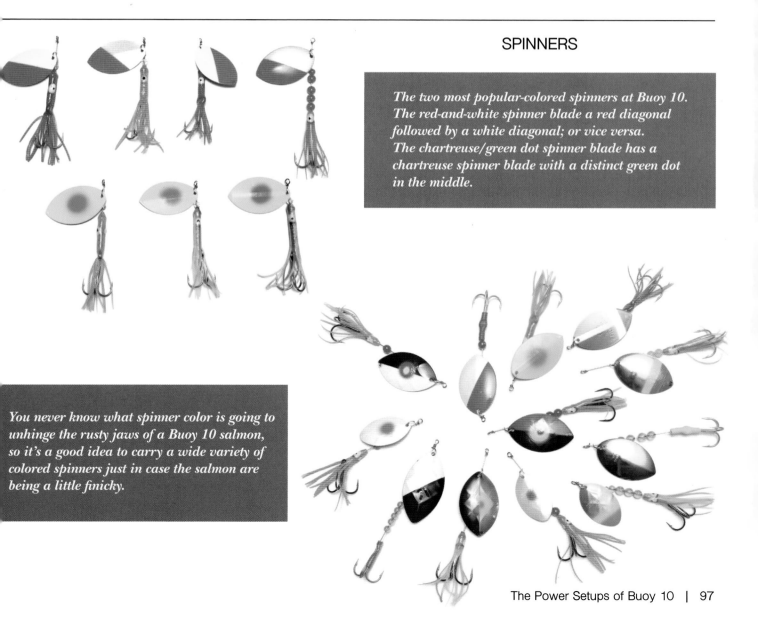

SPINNERS

The two most popular-colored spinners at Buoy 10. The red-and-white spinner blade a red diagonal followed by a white diagonal; or vice versa. The chartreuse/green dot spinner blade has a chartreuse spinner blade with a distinct green dot in the middle.

You never know what spinner color is going to unhinge the rusty jaws of a Buoy 10 salmon, so it's a good idea to carry a wide variety of colored spinners just in case the salmon are being a little finicky.

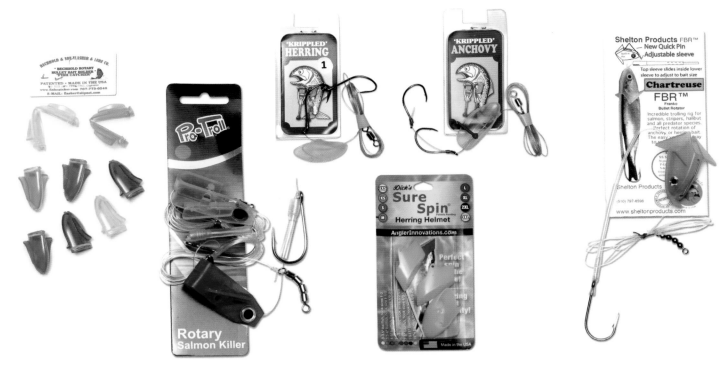

Some of the numerous nose cones available on the market.

40-pound monofilament for your leader.

I tie all my own mooching leaders because I like being able to choose my line, and I also have hook brand and style preferences. I usually run a 5/0 Gamakatsu or Owner octopus-style hook for my front sliding hook, and a 6/0 Gamakatsu or Owner octopus-style hook for the back hook. The back hook is attached to the back of the bait using a dental rubber band and I like to keep the curve of the hook just ahead of the baitfish's tail fin.

Slide down the nose cone of your choice onto the top hook, tie the leader to the end of the bead chain, rig-up a herring or anchovy and you are ready to fish.

I have used the Bechhold Rotary Bullet Bait Holder for over 10 years now with great success at Buoy 10 using both herring and anchovies.

For this particular bait holder, any color is good as long as it is chartreuse. I like to use a 4/0 or a 5/0 Owner SSW straight-eye hook for the front hook because the way the hole in the bait holder is situated,

the hook will always point away from the bait, looking very much like a fin. This helps to hook a lot of short-striking fish, or light-biting fish that are tending to nibble on the middle of the baitfish.

I will use either a 5/0 or 6/0 Owner or Gamakatsu octopus-style hook for the rear hook and either let it dangle or I will attach the baitfish to the hook using only a dental rubber band. I never pierce the baitfish with the back hook.

You can also use one single siwash hook using these particular baitfish holders if you so desire.

Rigging up is a snap. Run your leader out of the bait holder and tie it to a number 5 barrel swivel. Now you can attach either an Owner or a Gamakatsu siwash hook to the other end of the barrel swivel and let it dangle freely. The last step is to slide the head of a herring or an anchovy (anchovies work great for this rig) all the way inside the baitfish holder. A rubber band is used to keep the nose cone clamped shut.

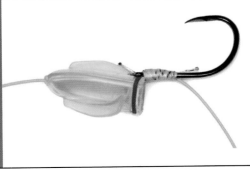

The first photograph shows how a straight-eye hook naturally faces outward from the bait holder, and the second photograph shows what the finished product should look like with the top hook inserted in the baitfish.

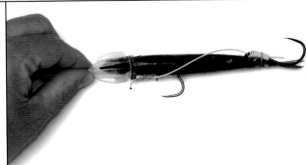

A rotary bullet bait holder using a single siwash hook.

CUT-PLUG HERRING

This fishery was born on cut-plug herring. If you want to run a cut-plug herring, tie a 2-hook sliding mooching leader using a 5- or 6-foot piece of 40-pound monofilament. Use either 4/0 or 5/0 hooks — for both hooks — based on whether you are using the smaller blue-label herring or the larger purple-label herring.

The bead chain that you have retrofitted at the back of the Fish Flash will normally be sufficient for taking out line twist, especially with the stiffer 40-pound monofilament. But some people still insist on putting another 6-bead bead-chain swivel about one-third of the way down the leader. Using two bead-chain swivels ensures that you will almost never get line twist.

Rigging-up a cut-plug herring is very easy. Insert the toe hook, or the rear hook, of your mooching rig into the herring first, about 1 inch or so into the high side of the herring, and then let the hook dangle freely, even with the tail of the herring.

Some people, including myself, believe it's more important what a herring looks like rather than what it smells like. But don't let your herring dry out; in between runs to various locations, store your cut-plug herring in the cooler so that it stays cool.

The most important thing about herring is that all of the scales are intact, and by all I mean every single scale. Herring with missing scales do not get bit as quickly as herring with all of their scales. For that reason, many anglers will not insert the rear hook inside the bait cavity. They insert the front hook alongside the spine of the herring about 1/2 an inch in back of the top portion of the slice, and they let the rear hook dangle freely without inserting it into the herring at all. This way the herring will keep all of its scales and look a lot more natural to the salmon.

Think about it. In the wild, herring have all of their scales. If a salmon were to see a herring missing even just one or two scales, it would look odd to them. It stands to reason that the herring with the most scales wins. For that reason, don't bother trying to hook the front hook directly into the spine of the herring, thinking that the herring will last longer. In the process of holding the herring very tightly, you will inadvertently knock a few scales loose. So the moral of hooking-up any baitfish, or plug-cut herring in this case, is to handle the fish with as few movements as possible. The person who can rig-up a herring the fastest is usually the person who will get the most hookups.

CUT-PLUGGING HERRING IN 6 EASY STEPS

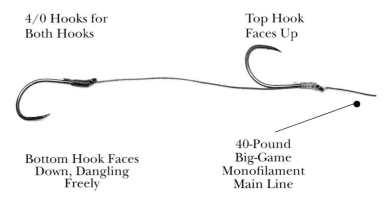

4/0 Hooks for Both Hooks

Top Hook Faces Up

Bottom Hook Faces Down, Dangling Freely

40-Pound Big-Game Monofilament Main Line

With either a fixed-tie or slip-tie mooching rig, it is a good thing if the top hook faces up and the bottom hook faces down in order to catch fish that are attacking your baitfish from all angles.

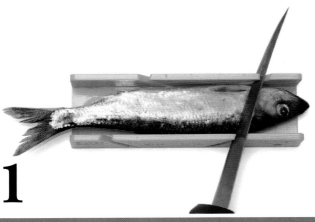

1

Step 1: Place the herring in your plug-cutter, with the back of the herring facing you.

Make sure you are using the chinook (king) slot of the plug-cutter. A plug-cutter normally has both a coho and a king slot for cutting different angles of the herring. Rest the rear end of your knife on top of the herring behind the gills.

2

Step 2: Pulling the knife toward you, make one continuous cut, slicing the head off at an angle.

4

Step 4: Vent the fish. Insert the tip of your knife inside the herring's exit hole and make a 1/4-inch slice toward the front of the herring. This will cause water to escape more easily through the fish's exit hole and cause less drag and damage to the herring while it is trolled.

5

Step 5: Insert the top hook about one-half inch behind the front of the herring so that the point of the hook slides along the backbone and comes out the top of the herring.

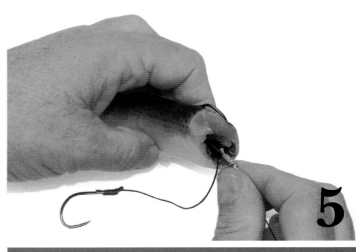

3

Step 3: Carefully remove the herring's guts with the tip of your knife.

6

Step 6: Let the back hook trail freely as a stinger. Make sure that the back shank of the hook is even with the back of the baitfish's tail so that you can catch those short-striking salmon.

Which brings me to a very important part of fishing any kind of baitfish. Make sure that you change your bait at least every 20 minutes. This means that you should have at least 2 trays of herring per person on the boat. The fresher and brighter the herring, the more fish you will catch.

CANNONBALL SINKER/WIRE SPREADER SETUP

With the barbless-hook regulation, a lot of anglers are using wire spreader setups utilizing a dropper with a cannonball sinker ranging from 10 to 16 ounces. I like to use some sort of wire spreader and keep the rigging simple. Luhr Jensen sells a wire spreader that works pretty well right out of the package. Here's how to rig-up.

Attach the corkscrew swivel at the end of your main line to the front end of your wire spreader. On a Luhr Jensen spreader, the shorter end is for the lead line, which is also called a dropper or dropper leader. Use 15-pound test for your dropper leader. The principle behind using only 15-pound test for your dropper is in the event that you should become snagged your lead line will break first, thus saving all your most expensive gear.

The lead line should be between 12 and 18 inches long, and that includes the length of the wire on the spreader. At the end of your dropper leader, tie a small snap to make it easier to attach the cannonball sinkers.

Attach the Fish Flash directly to the eye at the end of the spreader. On the end of your flasher, tie your 5- or 6-foot leader to a spinner, whole baitfish with a nose cone, or cut-plug herring.

This next part is very important.

When you let out the cannonball/wire spreader rig, let it out very slowly and only when the boat is in gear. If you let your lead line out too fast, or if you let it out while the boat has stalled, your cannonball sinker will tangle with your flasher.

I have had innumerable experiences using this rig with the best river guides in the business, and in rivers where this particular flasher was first born, and I can tell you with confidence that all the tangles involving the cannonball sinker and the flasher were due to letting the rig out too fast. Let this rig out very slowly, and only when you are at trolling speed, and you won't have any problems.

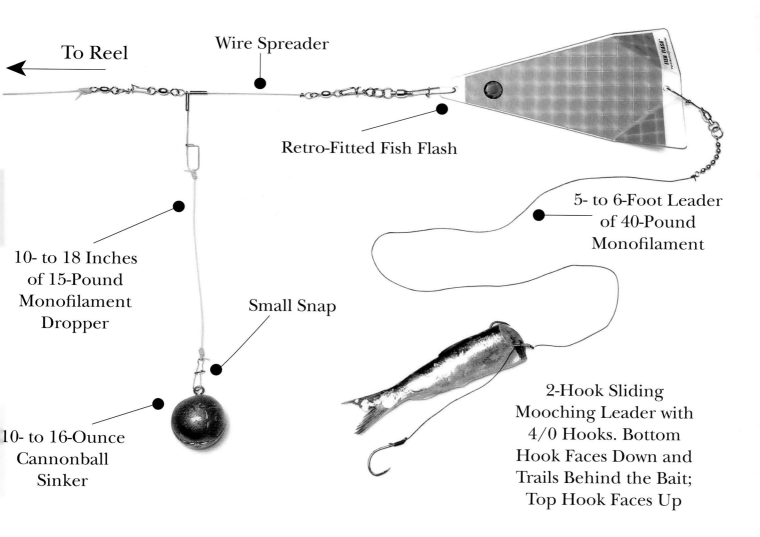

To Reel

Wire Spreader

Retro-Fitted Fish Flash

10- to 18 Inches of 15-Pound Monofilament Dropper

Small Snap

10- to 16-Ounce Cannonball Sinker

5- to 6-Foot Leader of 40-Pound Monofilament

2-Hook Sliding Mooching Leader with 4/0 Hooks. Bottom Hook Faces Down and Trails Behind the Bait; Top Hook Faces Up

A cannonball sinker/wire spreader outfit with a cut-plug herring attached.

SALMON BUNGEE

Some anglers use a Salmon Bungee between the end of the flasher and the beginning of the leader with a spinner or baitfish. The idea here is that with a piece of rubber tubing that can stretch up to three times its relaxed size salmon will be able to mouth the bait more without feeling any resistance.

I can tell you for a fact that these things do work, especially when trolling divers-and-spinners. I remember one particular trip back in 2009 when there were 5 people on the boat, four anglers were using Double Deep Six Divers leading to a Fish Flash. On the fifth rod, a Salmon Bungee was snapped onto the end of the flasher. A 5-foot leader was tied to the end of the Salmon Bungee and a size 6 1/2 Toman Thumper spinner in red-and-white was tied to the end of the leader. The rig is so simple to tie up and it's so deadly effective that I named it 'The Ultimate Red Setup For Coho and Chinook'.

It was a light's-out wide-open bite for coho, and quite a few wild coho were released. The chinook bite was on fire as well. At the end of the day, everybody limited out on chinook and coho, except for one angler who limited out on a chinook and a summer steelhead. Without exception, all of the fish were caught on rods using a Salmon Bungee and spinners.

I had never used a Salmon Bungee before this trip and I can say with confidence that they do exactly what they are supposed to do. If you're using the very long rods made for this fishery — the 10-1/2-foot sticks to the 12-foot monster rods — you may not need one because those rods should have enough cushion to allow chinook and coho to eat your bait without feeling any resistance. But if you have 2 or more people onboard your boat, it wouldn't hurt to have at least one rod out with a Salmon Bungee just to see if it fishes any better than the other sticks.

Larry Ellis's '*THE ULTIMATE RED SETUP FOR COHO AND CHINOOK*'

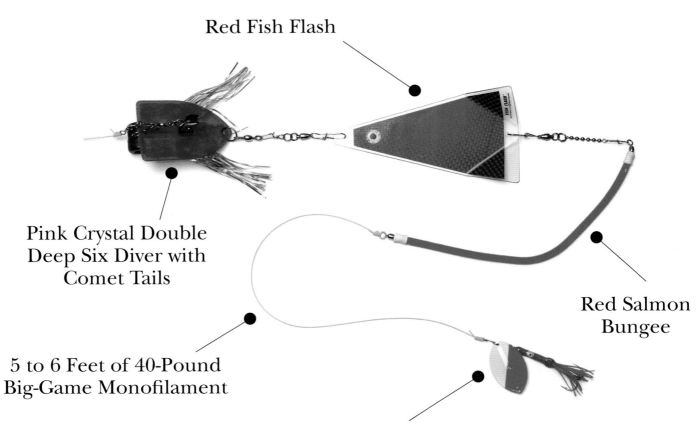

Red Fish Flash

Pink Crystal Double Deep Six Diver with Comet Tails

Red Salmon Bungee

5 to 6 Feet of 40-Pound Big-Game Monofilament

Size 6-1/2 Toman's Thumper Flex Squid Spinner in Luminous Fluorescent Red with a Hot Pink Squid Tail

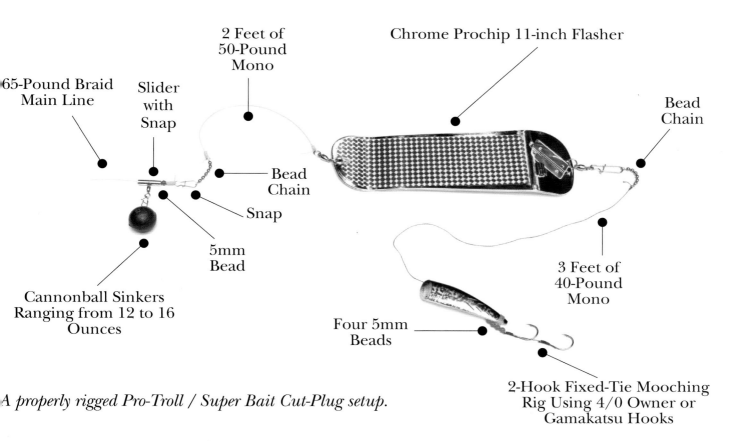

A properly rigged Pro-Troll / Super Bait Cut-Plug setup.

THE PRO-TROLL PROCHIP 11-INCH FLASHER WITH BRAD'S SUPER BAIT CUT-PLUG

Sometime in 2014-2015 anglers from the Hanford Reach brought one of their trade secrets to Buoy 10. The same outfit used to catch chinook like gangbusters in the Tri-Cities area of the eastern Columbia was tried out in the Buoy 10 arena.

The rig proved to be flat-out deadly, and this time-proven rig is now one of Buoy 10's best-kept secrets. Anglers should always keep a few on hand.

The rig uses an 11-inch Pro-Troll Pro Chip chrome flasher combined with a Brad's Super Bait Cut Plug. The Brad's lure looks exactly like a cut-plug herring and it doesn't really matter what color you use as long as you pack its bait compartment with oil-packed tuna. We're talking the least-expensive tuna you can find, so this is a very cost-effective setup. The oil-based tuna releases the tuna scent slowly, dispersing it via the oil through the water. It leaves a scent trail that no self-respecting salmon can resist, and it follows the oil-scented trail straight to your lure.

When a salmon's mouth engulfs this bait, there is no doubt about the hookup. It is a savage take-down in the most vicious manner.

The rig was so popular in 2015 that Pro-Troll could not keep enough of these flashers in stock. The company eventually ran out of them by the end of August. But fret not! Pro-Troll has made a point of making enough of these flashers for our future Buoy 10 excursions.

Pro-Troll's flasher works differently than any other flasher. When rigged properly, it makes a huge circle, imparting a wicked spin on the lure that both chinook and coho cannot resist! Add the scent of tuna to the equation and you have one of the hottest rigs known to man.

Make sure that you follow these directions precisely in order for the rig to work exactly the same way each time you go fishing.

Start with 65-pound braid for your mainline.

Use a slider with a snap attached directly to it; you can use any brand of slider. You will not be using a dropper in this setup. You can use a long plastic slider with a snap attached to the bottom or a very narrow plastic slider and then attach the snap to the hole in the bottom of the slider via the small end of a Duo-Lock snap. You can also use a brass slider, like the one shown in the picture below, that has a Duo-Lock snap attached to the hole at the bottom of the slider.

Slide the slider up the 65-pound braid mainline and then slide a 5mm plastic bead up the mainline. The bead will act as a cushion against the small end of a Duo-Lock snap. After tying your mainline to the small end of the Duo-Lock snap, snap a 6-bead bead-chain swivel to the large end of the same snap.

Now tie exactly 2 feet of 50-pound monofilament from the bead-chain swivel to the front end of the flasher. The length of this section is absolutely critical in order to get the precise circle of enticement that will attract salmon to your lure. Fifty-pound monofilament is used because your rig is only as strong as its weakest link. This way, if you break something off it will likely be your leader, which will be 40-pound monofilament, which will save your expensive, and sometimes unattainable, flasher.

The next step is to tie your leader, which will be 3 feet of 40-pound monofilament. Tie your hooks onto the leader first. There are many ways of rigging-up your hooks, but the fishermen who brought this rig to Buoy 10 preferred using a double or triple hook fixed-tie mooching setup using 4/0 Gamakatsu or Owner hooks. Do not forget to pinch the barbs off your hooks with a pair of needlenose pliers.

Slide down four 5mm beads onto the top hook of your fixed-tie mooching leader to keep the upper hook far enough away from the lure so the chinook can access that top hook.

If you are using a 2-hook mooching rig, keep the back hook spaced about one inch from the top hook.

Some people prefer using treble hooks somewhere in this leader setup, but others say that using a treble hook heavy enough for this fishery detracts from the action of the Super Bait Cut Plug. Just know that it is permissible to alter this rig slightly if you so desire.

Now, slide the upper end of your 3-foot leader through the proper spots on your Super Bait Cut Plug and tie the leader directly to another 6-bead bead-chain. Snap the bead chain to the back of the flasher.

Pick a cannonball sinker, ranging from 12 to 16 ounces, and snap it to the bottom of your slider. Pack the Super Bait with oil-packed tuna and you are

good to go — bombs away! Make sure that you can feel your sinker bouncing bottom on occasion to get in the zone.

TROLL AT LEAST ONE DEEP-DIVING PLUG
Most likely you will have a lot of people in your boat so, with one rod per angler, you can experiment using various setups until the salmon tell you what they want.

Many anglers have found that deep-diving plugs, especially the Mag Lip 4.5, have caught their fair share of chinook and coho. This particular lure works especially well in the Buoy 10 arena for several reasons. First of all, on a downstream troll with the current behind you it has the capability of running 20 feet deep when 40 feet of line has been let out. Since both the Washington and Oregon sides of Desdemona Sands have a slot that ranges from 20 to 25 feet deep, this is the perfect lure to flat-line directly off of 65-pound braid. Simply find this slot, let out 40 feet of line and you're in business!

A lot of people will use a 10-foot shock leader of 30- or 40-pound monofilament attached to the braid using a double UNI-Knot.

The Mag Lip 4.5 is also the perfect incoming tide lure when anglers hold their boats against the current or slowly let them slip upstream. With this technique the lure will not dive to 20 feet but will be fishing in a suspended mode. This is the perfect technique when fishing for suspended fish between 8 and 12 feet deep.

Five Mag Lip 4.5 lures known to catch salmon at Buoy 10. Starting from the top left and continuing clockwise, the colors are Thumper, Eradicator, Feeder, Fluorescent Red and Cerise Chartreuse Tigers, the latter two colors being extremely deadly on silvers. Make sure to pinch the barbs on all the Mag Lip hooks.

TIE YOUR OWN FIXED-TIE AND SLIP-TIE MOOCHING LEADERS

Why buy pre-tied fixed-tie and slip-tie mooching leaders when you can tie your own? The advantage of tying your own mooching leaders is that you can tailor-make them using any hook brand and style you wish and the freshest monofilament of your choice. You also have confidence knowing that your mooching rigs were tied by the best knot-tying master on the planet — you — not somebody thousands of miles away.

Tying fixed-tie and slip-tie mooching rigs is easy because you only have to learn one knot — the snell knot. If it is your first attempt at tying a snell knot, it won't take long to master. There are numerous types of snell knots, but the style used for these rigs is a very reliable and dependable knot and, in my opinion, it is the easiest knot to tie. I have tied mooching rigs using every knot known to man, but this snell is the strongest one that I have found in my 35 years of tying mooching leaders, and I have probably tied thousands of them.

Use 30- to 40-pound monofilament for the 4- to 5-foot leader for both the bottom and top hook of your fixed-tie mooching leader. And either 30-pound Dacron or 30-pound fly line backing to hold the upper sliding hook onto the leader of your slip-tie mooching rig using the same snell knot.

The photographs illustrate how these different rigs are tied.

Some people have trouble tying the upper sliding hook of the slip-tie mooching rig because they slide the top hook down the leader first. That's fine for tying a fixed-tie rig, but makes it difficult to insert the soft, flimsy line that will be holding the slip hook through the eye of the top hook because the hole in the eye is often very small.

By using my method, you will avoid this issue because you will be inserting the softer line through the hook eye of your top slip hook first, making it a breeze to insert the stiffer leader through the eye of the hook afterward.

You are also not limited to tying just two hooks with this rig. Where legal, people can tie up to a 3-hook mooching rig!

HOW TO TIE FIXED-TIE MOOCHING RIGS

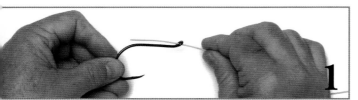

Step 1: Insert 30- or 40-pound monofilament leader through eye of an octopus-style hook.

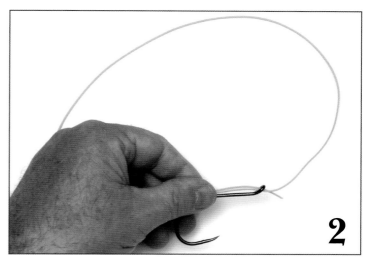

Step 2: While pinching the tag end of the line between your thumb and pointer finger, run the end of the leader about 1/2 inch through the eye of the hook going the opposite way. Pinch both pieces of line along the shank of the hook.

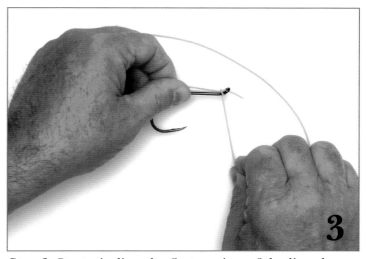

Step 3: Start winding the first section of the line down the hook shank over the tag end of the leader and the second section of leader.

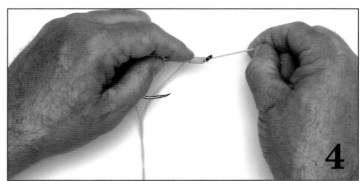

Step 4: Continue winding down the hook between 8 and 14 times, depending on the diameter of the line, and pull on the end of the leader until the loop in the hook is gone. Tip: turn the line clockwise while pulling on the leader to take out any line twist.

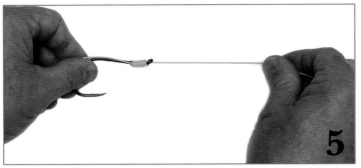

Step 5: Pull the leader tight until the wraps of the leader look tight and evenly spaced.

Step 6: Cut off the tag end of the leader about 1/4 inch from the end of the knot.

The second part of tying a fixed-tie mooching rig is tying the same knot for the top hook as you did for the bottom hook.

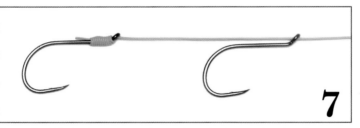

Step 7: Slide the second top hook down the leader until it is at the desired distance from the bottom hook.

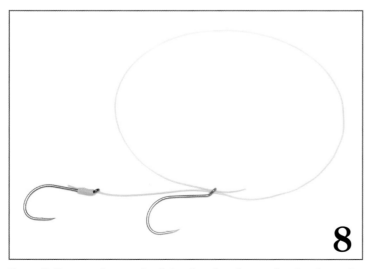

Step 8: Insert the end of the leader from the back end of the hook through the eye of the hook so that it comes out the front, just like in Step 2.

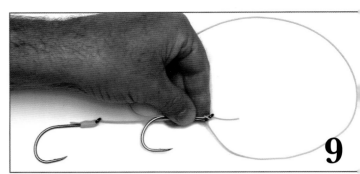

Step 9: While pinching the two sections of line onto the hook, start winding your line down the hook as in Step 3.

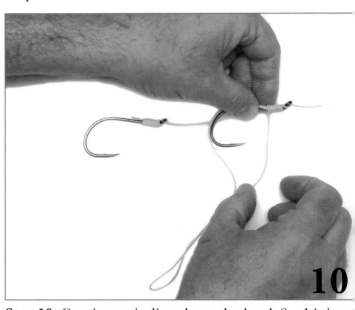

Step 10: Continue winding down the hook 8 – 14 times as in Step 4.

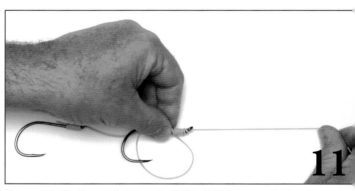

Step 11: Pull on the end of the leader until the loop gets smaller and finally disappears.

Step 12: Pull the end of the leader tight. Voila! You have tied a 2-hook fixed-tie mooching rig.

HOW TO TIE SLIP-TIE MOOCHING RIGS

Tying a slip-tie mooching rig is basically inserting line through the eye of the top hook and tying a snell knot, just as you did with the fixed-tie mooching leader. The only difference is that you will be inserting a 20-inch piece of either 30-pound Dacron or 30-pound fly line backing through the top hook eye first, in order to hold the top hook onto the single-hook rig that you made in Step 6 of the fixed-tie mooching rig.

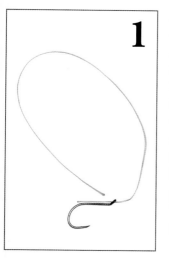

Step 1: Take a 20-inch piece of either 30-pound Dacron or 30-pound fly line backing and insert it through the eye of the hook so that the tag end hugs the shank of the hook, sticking out approximately 2 inches out the back of the hook. Now run the other end of the leader back through the hook eye going the opposite direction. This is the same as Step 1 of the fixed-tie mooching rig.

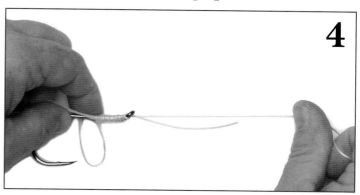

Step 4: Continue winding down the hook 8 – 14 times and then pull on the front of the 30-pound Dacron or 30-pound fly line backing until the loop gets smaller.

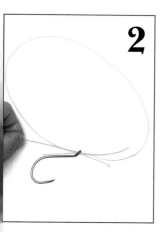

Step 2: Insert the front of your single-hook leader (that was made in Step 6 of the fixed-tie mooching rig) through the eye of the top hook, coming from the back of the hook and out the eye of the hook and extending about an inch or so out the front of the hook. You now have 3 pieces of line going through the eye of the hook.

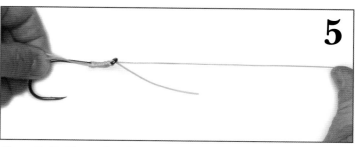

Step 5: Pull on the front end of the 30-pound Dacron or 30-pound fly line backing until the loop is completely out of the line, but do not pull this line very tight yet. Wet the leader and the new loops with water to lubricate the line and slide the top hook all the way down to the desired distance between the bottom hook and the top hook.

Step 3: While pinching all three pieces of line onto the shank of the hook, start winding down the shank of the hook starting just below the hook eye, using the first section of your 30-pound Dacron or 30-pound fly line backing. Keep the winds evenly spaced and not overlapping each other. This is basically a repeat of Step 3 of the fixed-tie mooching leader.

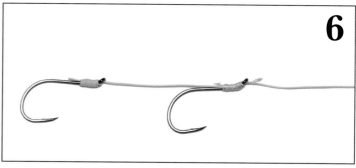

Step 6: When the top hook has reached the desired distance from the bottom hook, pull the 30-pound Dacron or 30-pound fly line backing tight until the top hook slides at your desired slip tension. Clip off all the tag ends and you are ready to fish a perfectly-tied slip-tie mooching rig.

Chapter 14

Buoy 10

Accommodations,

...Bait & Tackle

Everybody needs a place to lay their head and get plenty of the restorative sleep that will prepare them for the 3:00 a.m. wake-up calls and all the adventures that lay in store for them in the 14-mile expanse of the Buoy 10 Fishery.

For those who choose to overnight it in a motel, there are plenty to choose from in Astoria, Warrenton, Hammond, Ilwaco or Chinook. In addition to motels, folks can camp out at a fair number of campgrounds and RV parks as well. One friend of mine pulls his trailer and keeps it at an RV park where he has all the comforts of home, in addition to putting all his fillets or whole salmon directly in a freezer.

You must make your motel, campground or RV park reservations at least a year in advance. Fort Stevens State Park only takes reservations for the month of August during the month of November. If you wait until the middle of November, most likely the campground will be completely filled — and it is one big camping facility!

ASTORIA MOTELS

Astoria Crest Motel

(800) 421-3141; (503) 325-3141
5366 Leif Erickson Drive
Astoria, OR 97103
www.astoriacrestmotel.com

Astoria Rivershore Motel

(866) 322-8047; (503) 325-2921
59 W. Marine Drive
Astoria, OR 97103
www.astoriarivershoremotel.com

Astoria Riverwalk Inn

(503) 325-2013
400 Industry
Astoria, OR 97103
www.astoriariverwalkinn.net

Best Western Lincoln Inn Astoria

(503) 325-2205
555 Hamburg Avenue
Astoria, OR 97103
www.bestwesternastoria.com

Cannery Pier Hotel & Spa

(888) 325-4996; (503) 325-4996
#10 Basin Street
Astoria, OR 97103
www.cannerypierhotel.com

Comfort Suites Columbia River

(503) 325-2000
3420 Leif Erickson Drive
Astoria, OR 97103
www.comfortsuitesastoria.com

Hampton Inn & Suites Astoria

(800) 426-7866; (503) 325-8888
201 39th Street
Astoria, OR 97103
www.hamptoninn3.hilton.com

Holiday Inn Express Hotel & Suites

(888) 898-6222; (503) 325-6222
204 West Marine Drive
Astoria, OR 97103
www.hiexpress.com

Lamplighter Motel

(800) 845-8847; (503) 325-4051
131 West Marine Drive
Astoria, OR 97103
www.astoriamotel.com

Motel 6

(800) 441-3319; (503) 325-7111
288 West Marine Drive
Astoria, OR 97103
www.astoriadunes-motel.com

WARRENTON MOTELS

■ **Shilo Inn**

(800) 222-2244; (503) 861-2181
1609 E. Harbor Drive
Warrenton, OR 97146
www.shiloinns.com

HAMMOND MOTELS

■ **South Jetty Inn**

(503) 861-2500
984 Pacific Drive
Hammond, OR 97121
www.southjettyinn.com

CAMPGROUNDS AND RV PARKS FOR ASTORIA, WARRENTON AND HAMMOND

■ **Pier 38 RV Park**

(503) 836-2553
3738 Lief Erickson Drive
Astoria, OR 97103
www.facebook/pier38rvpark

■ **Lewis and Clark RV Park**

(503) 338-3386
92294 Youngs River Road
Astoria, OR 97103
www.lewisandclarkcampground.com

■ **Sunset Lake Resort and RV**

(503) 861-1760
33242 Sunset Beach Lane
Warrenton, OR 97146
www.sunsetlake.faithweb.com

■ **Kampers West RV Park**

(503) 861-1814
1140 NW Warrenton Drive
Warrenton, OR 97146
www.kamperswestcamping.com

■ **Fort Stevens State Park**

(800) 452-5687; (503) 861-3170
100 Peter Iredale Road
Hammond, OR 97121
www.oregonstateparks.org

■ **Astoria/Warrenton/Seaside KOA**

800-562-8506
1100 NW Ridge Road
Hammond, OR 97121
www.astoriakoa.com

■ **Hammond Marina RV Park**

(503) 861-0547
320 Lake Street
Hammond, OR 97121
www.facebook/Hammond Marina RV Park

ILWACO MOTELS

■ **Salt Hotel**

(360) 642-7258
147 Howerton Ave.
Ilwaco, WA
www.salt-hotel.com

■ **Col-Pacific Motel**

(360) 642-3177
214 First Avenue South
Ilwaco, WA 98624
www.colpacificmotel.com

■ **101 Haciendas Motel**

(360) 642-8459
Hwy 101 & Brumbach Ave. NE
Ilwaco, WA 98624

■ **Eagle's Nest Resort**

(360) 642-8351
700 W. North Head Road
Ilwaco, WA 98624
www.sunriseresorts.com

■ **Inn at Harbour Village**

(360) 642-0087
120 Williams Ave NE
Ilwaco, WA 98624
www.innatharbourvillage.com

Heidi's Inn Ilwaco

(800) 576-1032
126 Spruce St E,
Ilwaco, WA 98624
www.heidisinnilwaco.com

ILWACO RV AND CAMPING

Fisherman's Cove RV Park

(360) 642-3689
411 2nd Ave. SW
Ilwaco, WA 98624
www.ilwacofishermanscovervpark.com

Eagle's Nest Resort RV Park

(360) 642-8351
700 W North Head Road
Ilwaco, WA 98624
www.sunriseresorts.com

Cape Disappointment State Park RV

(888) CAMPOUT; (360) 642-3078
244 Robert Gray Dr.
Ilwaco, WA 98624

Beacon Charters & RV Park

(360) 642-2138
332 Elizabeth St.
Ilwaco, WA 98624
www.fishbeacon.com

River's End RV Park

(360) 777-8317
12 Bayview Street
Chinook, WA 98614

Deep River Camp

(360) 783-2638
9 Wainamo Road
Naselle, WA 98638
www.facebook/deeprivercamp

BAIT, TACKLE AND FISH PROCESSING

Yakima Bait Company

(509) 854-1311
www.yakimabait.com
Tackle manufacturer, flashers, spinners, plugs, you name it.

Sturgeon Paul's

(503) 861-2110
1080 Iredale St.
Hammond, OR 97121
www.facebook/sturgeonpauls
Bait, tackle, fish processing, vacuum packing, smoking.

Tackle Time Charters & Bait Shop

(503) 861 3693
Owner Gene Kane
530 E. Harbor St.
Warrenton, OR 97146
www.tackletime.net
Charters, tackle, frozen anchovies and herring, fresh anchovies and herring in the summer.

Wilky's Bait and Groceries

(503) 861-2088
1180 Pacific Dr.
Hammond, Oregon 97121
www.facebook/WilkysBait&Groceries
Frozen herring and anchovies, fresh herring in season.

Englund Marine

(503) 325-4341
95 Hamburg Ave.
Astoria, OR 97103
www.englundmarine.com
Incredibly-large supply of fishing tackle and supplies, rain gear, frozen bait.

Northwest Wild Products

(503) 791-1907
354 Industry St.
On the docks at The West Mooring Basin
Astoria, OR 97103
www.northwestwildproducts.com
Vacuum packing, filleting, fish processing, shipping.

Astoria Mini Mart

(503) 325-4162
95 W. Marine Dr.
Astoria, OR 97103
www.astoriaminimart.com
Frozen herring and anchovies, fresh bait in the summer.

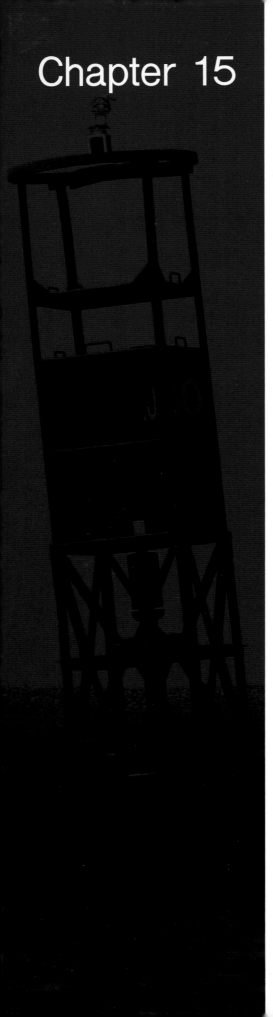

Chapter 15

The Future of Buoy 10

This fishery is growing by leaps and bounds, and it is not going to get any smaller. It's also limited — in the 14-mile stretch from the number 10 buoy up to Tongue Point/ Rocky Point — to approximately 31 days. It may last through Labor Day or be cut short suddenly due to quotas being met early.

I believe this fishery can be extended at least 2 weeks before the end of July through, at least, 2 weeks after Labor Day. During July, the tail end of the summer chinook season and the heart of the Youngs Bay SAB fishery are in full swing. Why not let us fish the estuary for those fish? Keep making more Select Area Brights and increase the release of fingerlings and smolts to 10 million fish. It can be done.

Toward the end of August and beginning of September coho are starting to grow to mammoth proportions. It is not uncommon to catch a coho at the beginning of September that ranges from 13 to 18 pounds, even approaching or exceeding the 20-pound mark.

Since the chinook fishery is winding down toward the end of August, and the retention of chinook is no longer allowed in the Buoy 10 fishery itself, why not increase the limit of coho to 3 fish instead of 2, to make up for not being able to catch chinook? I know a lot of people who would never consider traveling to Buoy 10 just to catch 2 coho, but they would gladly make the trip if they knew there was a possibility of taking home 3 coho, making up for not being able to catch a chinook. All that needs to be done to accomplish this would be to raise more fish in the hatcheries.

Changing the Buoy 10 fishery so that it starts around mid July and goes through mid September, or even longer, and allowing the retention of 3 coho toward the end of the fishery would extend a one-month fishery into a two-month fishery, possibly even longer.

I also believe that the hatcheries should go to 100% fin clipping of coho salmon. There are a lot of coho being caught in this fishery that are of hatchery origin but are not adipose fin clipped.

Then there's the problem with bumper-to-bumper traffic early in the morning. Since the local and global economy depends on this multi-million-dollar fishery Federal grant money surely could be raised to build more ramps, pave more parking lots, and build an extra lane on the Oregon side of the river to accommodate the extra traffic. One good grant writer could accomplish this goal.

This fishery is going to get bigger, not smaller. The population in the metropolitan area is growing every year, and a large portion of these people like to fish, and they like to fish in an area that's fairly close to home. In the not too distant future, we will be making reservations for motels, campgrounds and RV parks 2 years in advance.

In the next decade there will be an increase in angler trips during the Buoy 10 fishery, and there will also be an increase in fishing tourism from other countries. The future of Buoy 10 looks very promising, but we need to get down to work and find the answers now so that the mistakes of the past don't create problems in the future.